Make
West Virginia
No. 1

*What We Need to Know to
Make West Virginia the Most Prosperous
and All-Around Best State*

Make
West Virginia
No. 1

What We Need to Know to
Make West Virginia the Most Prosperous
and All-Around Best State

Defending Capitalism in a
Way that Everyone Can Support,
West Virginia Edition

By

Ralph William Clark

This book is for
Suzanne

I am indebted to George Bowles, Ted Drange, and Suzanne Clark for helping me to correct errors in earlier drafts of this book. Their help and advice are much appreciated. Any remaining errors are my own.

Table of Contents

Chapter 1.
West Virginia Can Be the Best

West Virginia has the potential to become the best state in the country—the most prosperous state and the all-around best place to live. In this book, I describe what needs to happen, and what West Virginia's voters need to know, in order for West Virginia to become the best state in the United States. Along the way, I discuss more broadly what the U.S. as a whole must do in order to become stronger economically and a better place to live. The most important thing that needs to happen is for voters everywhere to learn more about the true strengths of capitalism, regardless of the voters' political orientation—Democrat, Republican, Independent, liberal, conservative, or any other orientation. For this to happen, capitalism must be defended in a new way because none of the old ways is going to be convincing to a sufficient number of voters.

One of the major themes of this book is that capitalism has long been misunderstood and misrepresented. Nowhere is this more true than in West Virginia because of its unique history as a coal mining state.

A Negative Perception Of Capitalism

Mining of any kind is dangerous, coal mining especially so. Add in the fact that most coal mines are in rural, often isolated areas, as well as the fact that many West Virginia miners in the early 20th century were recent immigrants or first generation Americans whose prospects for employment were limited. It was more difficult for miners than for workers in other fields to pack up their families and change jobs in response to dangerous working conditions or low wages. This made it relatively easy for mine owners to take advantage of mine workers. One of the major consequences was a negative perception of capitalism on the part of numerous West Virginians.

From the perspective of the mine owners themselves, it could be said that the mining companies were responding to competitive pressures within the coal industry. But in the minds of many West Virginians, mine owners have long represented the institution of capitalism in a strongly negative light. It should not be a surprise that an anticapitalist mind set emerged many years ago in West Virginia. Events such as those leading up to the Matewan Massacre in 1920 and the ensuing Battle of Blair Mountain in 1921 helped to solidify this mind set. And it was not just coal mining that fostered a negative perception of capitalism. The history of economic development in West Virginia in the early 20th century in areas other than mining, such as the timber industry, also played an important role. Land owners, many of whom lived out of state, often seemed interested only in the money they could make quickly from timbering, leaving behind clear-cut land in poor condition.

Once in place, the anticapitalist mind set influenced West Virginia's political and economic policies during all of the remaining years of the 20th century and into the 21st century right up to the present time.

It was not only in West Virginia that anticapitalist ideas were gaining strength during those years. In the United States at large during the same period there existed—and still exist—powerful incentives for people in positions of power and influence to work against the dissemination of capitalistic ideas and ideals. As I demonstrate in this book, the value of capitalism lies in its beneficial effects on the economy of a state or a country *as a whole*. We should not expect that the interests, or perceived interests, of corporate leaders and elected officials will always be in agreement with the ideals of capitalism. Far from it, in fact, which is one of the reasons why capitalism has long been misunderstood and misrepresented. In later chapters, I discuss some of the major factors in business and government that count against having people learn the truth about capitalistic ideas and ideals.

By the end of this book I hope to convince you, if you are not already convinced, that people's lives go better when a society is more capitalistic. Compared to other types of economic incentives, the incentives belonging to free market societies are much more effective in motivating people to make the best choices leading to success and happiness, both for themselves and for others. This does not mean that people will always be treated well in capitalistic societies. West Virginians have experienced more than their share of hardships and mistreatment under an economic system that has possessed many of the elements of capitalism but at the same time has not fully lived up to the ideals of capitalism. The situation has not been helped by the sorts of things that politicians are fond of saying at election times, especially in West Virginia because of the longstanding anticapitalist mind set.

For many different reasons, the last one hundred years have not been kind to capitalism, either in West Virginia or in the United States at large. There has not existed an adequate communication to voters of important free market economic ideas. Yet, these same ideas could make a huge difference in strengthening both our state's economy and our national economy. All of these important ideas are spelled out in detail in this book.

West Virginia's Natural Advantages

There is no state in the country that can benefit more from capitalistic ideas than West Virginia. There are a number of reasons why this is so, including the fact that West Virginia possesses numerous natural advantages.

West Virginia is a wonderful state. It has an excellent climate—not too hot, not too cold, not too wet, not too dry. Hurricanes scarcely ever reach us with much destructive force. There are no major earthquake fault lines within the state, no volcanoes, relatively few tornadoes, virtually no large scale mud slides. West Virginia has a convenient, central location in relation to major cities such as Chicago, New York, and Atlanta, and its proximity to the Eastern seaboard is an important convenience as well. It is not difficult to drive from anywhere within West Virginia to beaches up and down the Atlantic coast. It is also not difficult to drive to numerous vacation areas in the parts of the Appalachian Mountains that lie to the north and south.

West Virginia itself has beautiful mountains, forests, rivers, streams, and lakes. It is rich in natural resources. Its people are industrious and friendly. It has a fine university system. Its crime rate is low by comparison to many other states, and so is its cost of living. Its interstate highway system is relatively new, and thus not in need of the hugely expensive repairs that currently face many other states.

Yet, for decades West Virginia has ranked at or near the bottom when it comes to most of the important measures of economic well-being, such as average income, life expectancy, quality of health care, and high school graduation rates. The percentage of people in poverty is higher in West Virginia than in most other states. In a ranking of "most livable states," posted online by Pearson Education, West Virginia is 45th among the fifty states. This ranking is based on a combination of factors such as household income, job growth, educational attainment, infant mortality rate, and unemployment. In recent years under Governor Joe Manchin, some progress has been made toward attracting more businesses to West Virginia and improving the quality of life for West Virginians. But the state has a long way to go. For 2009, for example, the U.S. Bureau of Economic Analysis placed West Virginia 47th in per capita income, an improvement from 49th place in 2008. In light of the fact that West Virginia possesses so many natural advantages, one might expect that our state would place much higher in many, if not all, of the important national rankings.

Changing The Anticapitalist Mind Set

What is the explanation for West Virginia's poor showing over so many years in regard to measures of economic well-being?

I believe that the anticapitalist mind set referred to above is the major culprit. It is not a coincidence that the most recent edition of *Economic Freedom of North America*, published by the Fraser Institute in 2010, assigns to West Virginia the lowest score among all the states for a composite measure of economic freedom. Although this ranking is for 2007, the most recent year for which comprehensive data are provided, there is no reason to believe that substantial improvement has occurred since then. I will be saying a lot in later chapters about what it means for a state or a country to possess economic freedom, and how the possession of economic freedom is undermined when people have an anticapitalist mind set.

Changing the anticapitalist mind set in West Virginia is a huge job.

One reason for this is that a great many people in the United States and around the world possess an anticapitalist mind set to one degree or another, not just West Virginians. The views of these people taken all together are very influential. They are to be found in business, government, news media, academia, and elsewhere. Many of these individuals sincerely believe that capitalism is deeply flawed as an economic system and as a way of life. If you count yourself among this group of individuals, then I urge you to read this book. I hope to change your mind, or at least to nudge you in the direction of changing your mind. This book is intended for other readers as well. In fact, this book is intended for everyone who wants to learn more about the strengths of capitalism, especially as they pertain to the U.S. economy, or about how to make West Virginia a much more prosperous state and a much better place to live.

Social and political forces have been in existence for a long time and in many different countries besides the United States that count against giving capitalism a fair hearing. For the most part, it is not the fault of voters in West Virginia, or anywhere else for that matter, that many of them are not in possession of the whole story regarding capitalism. This book is intended to provide the most important pieces to that story. I demonstrate that capitalism really can be defended in a way that appeals to people whose backgrounds and beliefs vary a great deal. Still, some people may be reluctant to read any book that defends capitalism.

The first thing that I want to say to individuals who are reluctant to put much time into reading "one more defense of capitalism that everyone has heard before" is that what I say in this book is *not* something that you will have heard before, at least not as a complete package of ideas. I do enumerate the major strengths of capitalism from classical sources. But I also address the shortcomings of capitalism, especially its moral shortcomings. One of the things that is unique about this book is the emphasis that I give to explaining how the *incentives of a capitalistic society* function in real world situations. I show how effective and encouraging are the incentives that belong to capitalism when properly understood. You may be surprised to learn just how much more effective and efficient are the incentives that belong to capitalism than are the incentives that belong to other economic and political systems. If West Virginia fully utilized these efficiencies, it would become the most prosperous state in the country and the most desirable state in which to live. Unemployment rates would decline a lot, while wages and salaries would increase a lot. If the United States as a whole fully utilized these same efficiencies, it would be able to dig itself out from under its present huge debt liabilities and greatly improve the quality of life for everyone.

With all of the laborsaving advances that technology has yielded during the last two centuries, from the industrial revolution to the computer evolution, people at the present time should not be struggling as much as they are, not in West Virginia, and not in the U.S. as a whole or in other countries. The key to improving life is economic and political reform.

Low Taxes, Least Red Tape, Highest Ethics

If West Virginia in the near future commits itself strongly enough to the reforms that I outline in this book, and carries through on those reforms, it will be in a position to describe itself as the state that has **Low Taxes, Least Red Tape, Highest Ethics**. I recommend that West Virginia adopt these words as a new, alternative state slogan (alongside Wild and Wonderful), and then work night and day to make this new slogan a reality: **Low Taxes, Least Red Tape, Highest Ethics**. This book lays a foundation for that to happen. It is not an unrealistic expectation in light of all of West Virginia's advantages.

West Virginia possesses an additional advantage that I have not yet mentioned. What I am about to say may seem paradoxical, but in reality there is nothing paradoxical about it: West Virginia's poor showing economically during all of the twentieth century and up to the present time can be put to good use to help us surge ahead in the future. Allow me to explain how this can happen.

Less Is More

Because West Virginia has for so long lagged behind most other states in terms of economic development, our present state budget and financial commitments are low by comparison to many other states. West Virginians have made do with less because we have had less. Government spending in West Virginia at the present time is large as a percentage of the state's economy compared to a lot of other states (and this fact in itself is economically unhealthy), but government spending is small in absolute terms for the size of our state because West Virginia is so poor. If West Virginia plays its cards right in the near future and becomes much more attractive to new and expanding

8

businesses, and to investors generally, it will experience very strong growth and a rapid increase in prosperity. Our state will be able to reduce substantially the proportion of government spending—thus helping to strengthen West Virginia's economic climate—while not needing to cut back on government services in order to get its house in order, unlike many other states at the present time which have greatly overextended themselves. In short, West Virginia has a lot of room within which to make up for past economic mistakes. And once it has done that, a more prosperous West Virginia will be able to increase its levels of public services and support for education in a responsible way that will not undermine its continuing prosperity. It will be able to repair its highways and bridges in a way that everyone will notice. It will be able to serve its people much better in numerous areas.

West Virginia has the potential to become the envy of other states. But we need to act fast. Numerous states across the country are also going to be working hard in the near future in their attempts to put their economic affairs in order as a response to the economically difficult times that people in the United States and around the world have experienced following the economic downturn that began in 2008.

The Strong Bond Among West Virginians

Can West Virginia do what needs to be done?

It will require a cooperative spirit within the state. But here, too, West Virginia enjoys a natural advantage when compared to other states, namely the fact that the people of our state share an unusually strong bond among themselves. More than the citizens of most other states, West Virginians enjoy a sense of shared solidarity which should enable us to pull together to make West Virginia number one among the states of the

Union—the best place to live, the best place to locate a business, the best place to invest, the best all-around state.

The first task that West Virginia faces is educational. As I mentioned above, in recent years the Manchin administration in cooperation with the state legislature helped to make West Virginia more business-friendly and a better place to live. These efforts need to be continued and expanded greatly; in later chapters, I explain how this can be done. But for progress to continue and to accelerate, West Virginia's voters need to understand what is at stake. If West Virginia is to become number one among the states of the union, its *voters all across the state* need to understand what must be accomplished in order to transform West Virginia. Otherwise, programs supported by one administration or by one or several legislative sessions can be weakened or undone by future governors or future legislative sessions.

West Virginians can and must help one another to gain the sort of understanding that is needed for genuine and long-lasting reforms to take place. If any state possesses what is required to accomplish this task, it is West Virginia.

Spreading The Word
(And Why This Book Is Needed)

This edition of *Defending Capitalism in a Way that Everyone Can Support* contains a clear, readable statement of essential capitalistic and moral ideas for making West Virginia the best it can be—hence the title, *Make West Virginia No.1*. (I should mention that I am currently working on another edition of *Defending Capitalism in a Way that Everyone Can Support* that is addressed more broadly to the United States as a whole.) I am not suggesting that what I say in this book is in any sense the last word, but I do believe that this book is a good beginning and is the best such book currently available. Some of the points that I make, especially regarding capitalism in relation to moral values, are absolutely unique to this book. My discussion of how these ideas apply to the special circumstances of West Virginia is also unique. Social and political forces in place for a long time have hindered the spread of capitalistic ideas and ideals. By contrast, informed voters will give us a rock solid foundation on which West Virginia can take a quantum jump forward. There exists no substitute.

If West Virginia is the first state to accomplish what I outline in this book, it will enjoy a strong advantage in regard to timing. It will set an example for the rest of the country. Being the first, it will garner a lot of attention, a lot of national press coverage, which means a lot of free publicity for all of the improvements that the state will be making in its efforts to implement **Low Taxes, Least Red Tape, Highest Ethics** on its way to becoming the best state in the union. When other states see how things are paying off for us, they will attempt to imitate some of the things that we are doing here. By getting there first, we will have positioned ourselves to stay ahead of the curve.

Chapter 2.
A New Direction for Capitalism

Question: What does the United States need at the present time more than anything else?

Answer: The U.S. needs a way to defend capitalism that large numbers of voters can accept and support—Democrats, Republicans, Independents, conservatives, liberals, and everyone else. The defense must be nonpartisan and nonideological insofar as possible. But this means defending capitalism in a new way because the old ways are never going to persuade sufficient numbers of people in all of the different groups. If the defense of capitalism does not reach out to enough people, we will all pay a high price.

American Debt

The amount of federal debt at the present time is almost unimaginably large and growing, and unfunded commitments to federal entitlement programs such as Social Security and Medicare are also huge and growing. At the end of fiscal year 2008 (September 30 of that year), the debt *interest* for the year was 451 billion dollars. The debt interest for fiscal year 2009 exceeded 500 billion dollars, and it will be larger still for 2010. But the only good option in any country for dealing with a huge national debt and other financial commitments is for the country as a whole to make a lot of money by having a strong economy, while simultaneously taking steps to control government spending. The way to have a strong economy is to implement all of the best capitalistic reforms. This will allow us to earn our way out of our present financial difficulties.

If the United States does not begin immediately to make itself more competitive and a better place to do business, it will sink under the weight of its debt. Our standard of living will decline, and everyone's opportunities for success and happiness will shrink. The United States absolutely must do everything it can to create a strongly robust economy, and there is no time to lose.

Let us take the lead in West Virginia!

The best way for us to take the lead is to implement **Low Taxes, Least Red Tape, Highest Ethics** for our state.

As citizens of the United States, we need to act fast because numerous countries around the world will be working hard in the near future to put their own economic affairs in order. We must lower taxes and cut back on spending, especially at the federal level. We must simplify the steps that are taken when a new business complies with governmental rules and regulations, or when an existing business expands. We must simplify the requirements for filing tax statements and complying with any and all of the rules and regulations that affect the day-to-day operations of a business—not to mention the task of getting on with our lives apart from business. We must make government user-friendly at all levels.

As residents of West Virginia, we have a unique opportunity to set an example for the rest of the country. The more that we can be leaders, not followers, the more we will benefit.

A New Direction

In this book, I describe a "new direction for capitalism" that places capitalistic ideas and ideals on a solid foundation that is both economic and ethical. My New Direction for Capitalism (which I also refer to as NDC) contains a more comprehensive moral defense of capitalism than readers will find elsewhere, and a new and better way for readers to understand the economic strengths of capitalism, as well as the limitations of capitalism. My goal is to reach out to everyone who wants to do their part to make West Virginia the number one state in the United States, and to ensure that the United States itself remains the great country that it has always been.

In order to help readers understand better what I mean by my New Direction for Capitalism, I turn now to a brief account of how I began my own journey toward understanding the economic and moral foundations for NDC.

Ayn Rand And Lyndon Johnson

When I was sixteen, like many young people of my generation, I read Ayn Rand's *Atlas Shrugged* and *The Fountainhead*. *Atlas Shrugged* had been published a few years earlier, and was much talked about at the time. I was captivated by Rand's vision of capitalism because it seemed so pure and elegant. In the ideal society as described by Rand, everyone would do their best to make the most of their lives while government would leave people alone to find their way in the world. According to Rand, the best life is the most productive and creative life, governed by the rational minds of individuals pursuing their own self-interest within a capitalistic society. The most memorable

15

message that I got from Rand was that "rugged individualists" are the true movers and shakers in history. Entrepreneurs are heroic. I was enthralled as well by Rand's tribute to the life of the mind. I was intrigued by Rand's message that people's ideas make a huge difference in their lives in determining whether the people end up being happy or successful. I was already interested in ideas myself.

A few years later, when I was an undergraduate at the University of Denver in the 1960s, I began to read newspapers carefully for the first time in my life. There were stories about the Civil Rights movement in the South, impoverished communities in Appalachia, unemployment and unrest in big cities, victims of earthquakes and floods in Asia, victims of bigotry all around the world. The fact that millions of people lived excruciatingly difficult lives was something of a revelation to me, and I told myself: People must help one other. Nothing is more important than the concern that each of us can show for those in need and for the well-being of society as a whole. I saw more clearly that people should not be wholly self-interested, contrary to the view of Ayn Rand. I switched my allegiance from Rand's Objectivism to Lyndon Johnson's Great Society.

At about the same time, I began to take philosophy classes from Professor Leonard Peikoff, then at Denver, a captivating lecturer who knew Ayn Rand personally. Peikoff later wrote several books about Rand's ideas and helped to found the Ayn Rand Institute. I switched majors from English literature to philosophy. I read Henry Hazlitt's *Economics in One Lesson*, published in 1946, and Milton Friedman's *Capitalism and Freedom*, published in 1962. I learned more about the huge inefficiencies that so often result when governments attempt to help people in need, and when governments intervene in the world of business for other reasons as well. I acquired a better understanding of the crucial role that competition plays in the world of business, and the great importance of private property and free trade.

Once again, I became an enthusiast for Rand's defense of capitalism, but with a major difference this time. I was attracted to her political and economic philosophy of free markets under capitalism and limited government, but I could not reconcile myself to Rand's defense of the moral philosophy of egoism, nor could I accept Milton Friedman's related view that the only moral responsibility of corporate managers is to make as much money as possible for their stockholders within the legal boundaries of a capitalistic society. I was beginning to see much more clearly that Rand and Friedman tie their defense of capitalism to a viewpoint that is morally unacceptable. (In later chapters, I spell out exactly why it is morally unacceptable.) Friedman's *Capitalism and Freedom*, for example, contains clear statements of many important economic ideas and has helped to educate a lot of people about the strengths of capitalism. But it also contains the following unfortunate passage, which has been widely quoted:

Few trends could so thoroughly undermine the very foundations of our free society as the acceptance by corporate officials of a social responsibility other than to make as much money for their stockholders as possible.

The American Capitalistic Ideal

While many different factors have contributed to making the United States a great country, the most important has been the extent to which, since its founding, the United States has supported a free enterprise economic system, otherwise known as capitalism. Yet, capitalism is widely criticized at the present time, and always has been subjected to varying

17

degrees of criticism throughout our country's history. After two and a quarter centuries, during which time the United States has been an immensely successful nation, the American capitalistic ideal is still not widely enough accepted as constituting a genuine ideal. Large numbers of Americans do not accept it, and even larger numbers of people in other countries do not accept it.

Not only is capitalism not widely *perceived* to be a genuine ideal, but the government of the United States has been *actively engaged* in moving the country away from free market ideas. Nothing typifies this movement more than the fact that the national debt was $5.7 trillion at the end of the 2001 fiscal year, but now is more than $13 trillion. Although a substantial portion of the increased debt was incurred during the administration of President George W. Bush, and was seen then to be a huge problem by a substantial number of voters and opinion-makers, the rate of increase is not slowing down at the present time. Quite the contrary, in fact. The deficit is being run up as a consequence of the federal government's economic interventions and a myriad of spending projects. Even some of the severest critics of capitalism believe that President Obama and Congress are going too far in their incursions against capitalism. The results of the November 2010 elections, held just as this book was being completed, giving Republicans control of the U.S. House of Representatives, suggest that many American voters share this assessment.

What is missing, however, is any sort of genuinely broad-based and principled support for capitalism that recognizes its limitations, and any sort of broad-based repudiation of the major criticisms and misrepresentations of capitalism that have been in the air for many years and have intensified during the present economic downturn and partial recovery from the economic downturn. There is no getting around the fact that the American capitalistic ideal is in trouble.

What has happened?

Capitalism Has Acquired A Bad Reputation, Partly Deserved

In the minds of many people, the defense of capitalism has long been intermeshed with the idea that capitalism encourages the unrestrained pursuit of profit in the world of business. My references above to Rand and Friedman illustrate this connection. In her writings, Rand calls herself an egoist and urges others to become egoists. Friedman does not defend egoism, but he does defend the idea that the one and only goal of every business or corporation should be to make a profit. For Friedman, the pursuit of profit in business within the context of a free market economy should not be compromised by any other goals. This "pure profit seeking" model for business is not acceptable. In later chapters, I demonstrate that capitalism absolutely does not need to be, nor should it be, tied to egoism or to the idea that the only goal of business should be to make a profit.

Yet, the fact remains that capitalism has acquired a bad reputation in the minds of a great many people. This reputation is partly deserved because numerous individuals in business do engage in the unrestrained pursuit of profit. The actions of such individuals are sometimes defended by "appeals to capitalism." Even when businesses are run completely morally, there exists guilt by association. Thus, a great many people in the United States and other countries tell themselves that the following is true: Capitalism is based on an inadequate moral philosophy (namely, something like Rand's egoism or Friedman's pure profit seeking prescription), so there must be something inherently wrong with capitalism and capitalists. The U.S. ought to be moving in the direction of becoming less capitalistic, not more capitalistic, these people say. Indeed, many people believe that capitalism is so problematic that even a flawed "case for capitalism" is not worth making. When such individuals are in positions of influence—as teachers, professors, journalists, newscasters, pundits, politicians, novelists, screen writers, and others—their views are passed on to even greater numbers of individuals who, as a consequence, remain partially or wholly uninformed about the great strengths of capitalism. This is an extremely unfortunate situation because the economic reforms that are so much needed in West Virginia, the United States as a whole, and countries around the world will not take place or remain in place unless a large majority of voters gain a sufficient understanding of the true strengths of capitalism.

Therefore, as I said earlier, what the U.S. needs most at the present time is a view of capitalism that a large majority of voters can support, regardless of their political orientation. West Virginia is in need of exactly the same thing. People everywhere need a basis for overcoming the partisan divisions that presently rob our political and social lives of so much energy. We need a way to come together in support of what is best for our state and our country.

Rather than rejecting capitalism because of its association with moral ideas such as those of Rand and Friedman, people should conclude instead that capitalism needs to be defended in a new and better way on the basis of moral ideas that *are* acceptable, and that also encompass the limitations of capitalism. Nothing else will make it possible for the U.S. to dig itself out from under its huge debt, and for capitalism to play its proper role in increasing the likelihood that most people will end up living successful and happy lives. Nothing else will make it possible for capitalistic ideas to play the role that must be played if West Virginia is to become the highly prosperous state that it has every reason to become. Nothing else will enable people everywhere to benefit fully from all of the technological advances that have occurred during the past two centuries.

Capitalism, when properly understood and defended, is a political, economic, and moral ideal whose time has come. Indeed, a stronger defense for capitalism is possible today than ever before. There are several reasons why this is so.

Why The Case For Capitalism (When Properly Understood) Has Become Stronger

Many important economic lessons have been learned. The first reason why the case for capitalism is stronger now than in the past is that a lot has been learned during the past century about the real world economics of competition, government planning, economic regulation, banks and currency, welfare programs, health care, and other issues that are relevant to the defense of capitalism. For example, America experienced the Great Depression of the 1930s, which taught many important lessons (of course, not everyone learned those lessons—I discuss some of them later on). We are now experiencing the effects of another economic downturn, with the potential for teaching additional important lessons. Likewise, Americans have accumulated a lot of valuable experience as regards government welfare programs. The overall success of welfare reform legislation passed in 1996 during the Clinton administration has taught valuable lessons. Much is being learned at the present time about health-care delivery systems. Much is being learned about what happens when various sorts of aid are given to foreign countries. Much has been learned about trade policies. In all of these areas, and numerous other areas as well, it is crucial that people

21

draw the right conclusions as to what works, what is counter-productive, and what passes muster on moral grounds. We must look carefully at both the intended and the unintended consequences of economic policies in the areas just mentioned, and the same is true regarding tax systems, currency and inflation, accounting practices for corporations, regulation of the stock market, and so on. All of the knowledge now accumulating can and must be put to good use. This will not happen fully if the defense for capitalism is not thoroughly reinvigorated on the basis of moral considerations as well as economic and political considerations.

Large-scale moral improvement has occurred within the U.S. and many other countries. The second reason why a stronger defense for capitalism is possible today than ever before is that, especially during the last fifty years, a great many Americans, along with large numbers of people around the world, have undergone a process of "consciousness-raising" in regard to matters of race, gender, class status, and other dimensions of how people interact with one another. Much more than in the past, people now see each other essentially as human beings, and not primarily as members of a particular race, or as men vs. women, or in some other way as "them" vs. "us." There is a new attitude of respect for, and concern about the well-being of, minorities, women, the handicapped, the elderly, the mentally ill, children, gays and lesbians, and other individuals who suffered from discrimination, abuse, or neglect in the past. This new moral outlook is one of the most important legacies of the 20th century.

As a consequence, it is much easier now than ever before to defend the idea that capitalistic government should, for the most part, leave people alone to set their own course through life, just because so many people at the present time are more inclined than in the past to treat all of their fellow human beings with respect and concern. More consciousness-raising is needed, of course, as regards race, gender, religion, and other dimensions of life, but a lot of moral progress has been made. The greater extent to which people now express goodwill toward their fellow human beings, as the result of the consciousness-raising that has taken place, means that the defense of economic freedom under capitalism (when capitalism is properly understood) is that much easier.

In years past, it was inevitable that groups suffering from discrimination would not appreciate the strengths of the capitalistic system in place at the time. The number one strength of capitalism has always been that it constitutes the best overall economic and political system when compared to the alternatives. Capitalism lies in the background, so to speak, while the circumstances of one's own life lie in the foreground. Understandably, it is difficult for someone to focus on the comparative strengths of a system that lies in the background when the group with which one identifies most strongly—women, African Americans, the elderly, the handicapped, etc.—is being discriminated against to such an extent that the major benefits of the system seem to be lost to members of the group in question. An American woman in the 1960s, for example, who was kept out of graduate school in the sciences just because she was a woman, as many were, understandably had difficulty appreciating the type of capitalistic system in place at that time. An African American living under Jim Crow laws prior to 1965, or subject to continuing racist attitudes in years following 1965, understandably had difficulty appreciating the type of capitalistic system in place at the time. Human beings are not naturally inclined to carry through on the extensive processes of abstraction required in circumstances such as these in order to see that capitalism is still a good system overall even if one's own lot is not so fortunate and the group to which one belongs is being treated unfairly.

The really good news at the present time is that the moral consciousness-raising to which I am referring has changed things a great deal within all of the states of the United States and within many countries around the world as well: The members of disadvantaged groups can now much more thoroughly and frequently experience for themselves the same benefits from capitalism that members of other groups have always enjoyed. Thus, as I said, it is much easier now than in the past for capitalism to be defended. Indeed, a new era is about to begin if we take the steps necessary to bring it into existence: An era of "post-twentieth century capitalism." I am talking about a new and much improved version of capitalism that is a beneficiary of all the "rights movements" of the second half of the 20th century, plus other improvements. My New Direction for Capitalism is intended as a road map to this new era.

The Downside Of Moral Consciousness-Raising

Before leaving the subject of moral consciousness-raising, I need to address a *negative* consequence that bears upon the defense of capitalism. This negative consequence constitutes the second part of my answer to the question raised above, Why is the American capitalistic ideal in trouble at the present time? (The first part of my answer is that capitalism has acquired a bad reputation that is partly deserved.)

As I just mentioned, there is at the present time in the U.S. and many other countries a new attitude of respect for, and concern about the well-being of, minorities, women, the elderly, the handicapped, gays and lesbians, and other individuals who have suffered from discrimination in the past. This new attitude of respect is one of the most important legacies of the twentieth century, as I said. The downside to the emergence of this new attitude is that it has led many people to continue to call upon government to play an ever larger role in human affairs, not the smaller role that is required at the present time if capitalism is to be reinvigorated. Advocates of having government play larger and larger roles frequently say something along the following lines: If people truly are concerned about one another, then that is what really matters. Goodwill is what matters. The world does not need limited, capitalistic government. In fact, because benevolent actions are so important, the power of government ought to be invoked very extensively on the side of helping those in need, making the world a better place overall, and/or promoting greater equality among people. In all of the efforts to help people in need, many people say, capitalism is more a hindrance than a support.

What these people should conclude instead is that we need government to become more capitalistic in order to protect economic freedom and allow people to set their own course through life and to strengthen the economy, but we *also* need a clear recognition that there exist strong, positive moral obligations to one's fellow human beings. These positive obligations, should in a *limited way* be invoked in defense of government programs and legislation for helping people in need and making society better overall.

What is crucial for the present time is that positive moral obligations not be invoked to enlarge the sphere of government to such an extent that any of the major benefits of capitalism are jeopardized. Let me repeat: We must not allow the major benefits of capitalism to be jeopardized. But they will be jeopardized if we do not undertake major reforms to make government much less expensive and burdensome, yet more ethical as well. When government provides welfare support for people who cannot help themselves, for example, such support must be given in ways that really work because they take into account basic facts about human psychology and motivation. The need for welfare programs or other types of government support must not be used as a stepping stone for making government continually larger and larger. This caution applies also to the appropriate roles that government should play in ensuring that everyone has access to health care, has an adequate pension when retired, and does not suffer from discrimination on the basis of race, gender, religion, disability, or sexual orientation. I say more in later chapters about the appropriate "helping roles" and "protecting roles" that government should play in an era of post-twentieth century capitalism.

Blaming Capitalism Unfairly For Economic Hard Times

There is also a third part of my answer to the question raised above, Why is the American capitalistic ideal in trouble at the present time? I discuss this part of the answer at length in Chapter 4. In a nutshell, what I say in Chapter 4 is that because so many people in the United States and other countries possess an inadequate understanding of capitalism, these same people assign to capitalism much more blame than is justified when an economic crisis occurs, such as the severe economic downturn that began in 2008. The resulting linkage in people's minds between capitalism and the occurrence of economic crises causes people to pay even less attention than they might otherwise pay to efforts by pro-capitalist writers to defend capitalism. As a consequence, the defense of capitalism—especially the sort of defense that is clear and compelling to large numbers of voters and opinion-makers, which is exactly what West Virginia, the

United States as a whole, and the world at large so desperately need at the present time—remains elusive.

What can be done to turn this situation around?

Answer: We need an analysis of recent and not-so-recent economic history that properly assigns blame for economic crises to *both* the capitalistic and the non-capitalistic elements in the political and economic systems of countries like the United States. I present such an analysis in Chapter 4.

Who Should Read This Book?

If you are someone who already believes that capitalism is a good thing, and especially if you are frustrated by the extent to which capitalism is criticized and undermined in today's world, then this book is for you. My main goal is to convince you that capitalism as I defend it, namely my New Direction for Capitalism, has the potential for being much more strongly supported in today's world than any other version of capitalism. I want to convince you that, in the domain of economic, political, and moral ideas, NDC is the world's best realistic ideal. It is best for West Virginia, the United States as a whole, and the world at large.

If you are someone who at the present time has more sympathy for the critics of capitalism than for its supporters, then this book is for you as well. I hope to change your mind, or at least to nudge you in the direction of changing your mind. My goal is to demonstrate to you that NDC really is everyone's best bet for achieving success and happiness.

NDC is what a country like the United States needs in order to maintain and strengthen its competitive edge within the world's economy. NDC is what a state like West Virginia needs in order to strengthen its competitive edge within the country as a whole. The really good news for West Virginians, as I mentioned in Chapter 1, is that our state is especially well-placed to benefit from the right sorts of capitalistic reforms.

The key to understanding those reforms is understanding how the incentives of capitalism motivate people to be successful. The economic incentives that exist within a society, whatever form they may take, are always present, nudging people in successful directions or in not-so-successful directions. Therefore, having the right sorts of incentives in place in a state or country is extremely important. In the next chapter, I discuss some of the steps that must be taken in order to create the very best economic incentives.

Chapter 3.
Incentives Make the World Go Round

Nothing is more important for the economy of a state or country than having in place the best incentives for people to be successful in business. I will first say a few words about incentives in general.

Whatever it is that people end up doing in their lives, incentives are always present that play a large role in getting people to act. Incentives are motivators. Incentives can get people to make the right choices—or the wrong choices—depending on what the incentives happen to be. Some incentives are internal, such as hunger pangs which provide a person with an incentive to find something to eat. Another example would be when I feel thankful for a kindness that someone has shown me; I have an incentive to express my appreciation. I have an incentive *not* to do something if I believe that doing it is morally wrong. Internal incentives consist either of feelings or beliefs, or a combination of the two.

External incentives are more difficult to pin down. Fortunately, as far as this book is concerned we do not need to look at external incentives in their entirety but only at the most important ones, namely economic incentives. There are two main types of economic incentives: those belonging to the private sphere of business, and those belonging to the public sphere of government. For example, if I learn that a particular store has the best price for an appliance that I need, I have an incentive to visit that store. When I receive a tax bill with penalties for not paying on time, I have an incentive to make a prompt payment. If new taxes are imposed that take away a larger percentage of the profits that I make in a business that I run, I have weaker incentives than before to expand the business, or even to go on running the business at all. If I must pay higher capital gains taxes, I have weaker incentives to invest in real estate or stocks because I will receive a smaller return as compensation for the risks that I take in making such investments.

At least most of the time, we act on the basis of whatever happens to be the strongest overall incentive or combination of incentives present to us. I have included the words "at least most of the time" in the previous sentence because I want to leave room for the existence of human free will. If free will exists (I believe that it does, but defending my belief in free will is beyond the scope of this book), it allows us sometimes to choose not to act on the basis of the strongest incentives that face us on a particular occasion. In other words, human beings are not like puppets or robots, at the complete mercy of all the different incentives, or motivators, that they face in their lives. Human existence is more complex than that. However, even when free will operates, incentives are still extremely important. We can still say that incentives make the world go round because it remains true that most of the things that people do are largely determined by the incentives that people experience. Day in and day out, incentives play a crucial role in our lives. This is true whether we are talking about internal incentives, such as moral beliefs, or external incentives, such as those bearing upon the likelihood that a business venture will be profitable. Most people in today's world face numerous incentives throughout their lives that motivate them to be productive members of society, but they also face far too many incentives that motivate them in exactly the opposite direction.

A person's life can have a lot of potential, but unless the person experiences the right sorts of incentives at the right times, success and happiness may never be achieved, or achieved only to a very limited extent.

The Incentives Of Capitalism—Everyone's Best Bet For Success And Happiness

Over the last three centuries, an increasingly strong case has emerged in defense of the idea that the incentives of capitalism are the most important external incentives for making people's lives go better. These incentives have to do with several different features of capitalism, but especially the fact that capitalism emphasizes competition and private property. Competition in the workplace motivates people, on the whole, to do their best to please customers, clients, employers, employees, investors, and others. Likewise, when land, resources, capital, or other property is owned privately by individuals, these individuals are motivated, on the whole, to do their best to put their property to good use in pleasing people. Investing money in a business always entails risk, which provides a strong motivator for investors to learn all they can about the likelihood that a business will be successful. The most important factor in making a business successful is pleasing the people whom the business serves.

Competition drives down prices and improves quality because it allows consumers to engage in comparative shopping.

Whenever a consumer makes a purchase on the basis of price, safety, durability, convenience, or some other factor, a "marketplace vote" is cast for that particular feature of a product or service. Anyone who wants to run a successful business must pay a lot of attention to the results of consumer voting. Thus, competition and private property motivate people and companies to produce better goods and services at lower prices, and to use resources and facilities in the most effective ways for producing the best things at the best prices. Likewise, whenever someone invests wisely in a company, or in resources, technologies, commodities, and so on, there is always the expectation that the greatest profits will be made where there is the greatest likelihood of success by people who pay close attention to consumers' votes. People who work for a successful company but do not have an ownership stake in the business normally can expect that their wages or salaries will, at least to some extent, reflect their contribution to the company's success.

The control over our money that we exercise through ownership is crucial as an incentive where wages and profits are concerned for the obvious reason that no one will be strongly motivated to work hard at their job or take risks when investing their savings if most of the money that they expect to earn will be taken from them through taxes, or if there is little that they can do with the money that does remain in their possession. Everyone's primary motivation for earning money is to be able to do what they want with it.

Does this mean that capitalism makes people selfish, or that people must already *be* selfish, in order for capitalism to work properly? Many critics of capitalism insist that the answer is yes to both parts of this question. But in reality the correct answer is *no* to both parts. People who have a large measure of control over their money can choose to spend it for selfish reasons but they can also choose to spend it for non-selfish reasons. In both types of situation, people have a stronger incentive to earn money if they have greater control over their money, regardless of whether they earn the money from their jobs or by making profitable investments. Under capitalism, people have much more control over their money than they do under any other type of economic system.

West Virginia

How do the points that I have been making apply specifically to West Virginia?

When it comes to attracting new businesses and investments, if our state makes a series of small improvements to the economic incentives that exist here, such as the improvements achieved during the Manchin administration, we can expect that there will be small but significant improvements in the economic well-being of West Virginians. The more that West Virginia's voters understand how capitalism works, and the more that people inside and outside of the state perceive that West Virginia's voters understand how capitalism works, the more enduring will be these improvements.

However, if West Virginia is to take full advantage of its natural strengths, the improvements need to be large enough that West Virginia comes to be seen as being substantially better than a lot of other states, not just a little better than it was in the past. As I mentioned in Chapter 1, West Virginia has a long way to go in its efforts to become an economic leader among the fifty states because of the decidedly business-unfriendly climate that our state has fostered for so many years—a climate caused in part by the long-standing anticapitalist mind set in West Virginia. The challenge that faces us now is to cross the magic threshold where West Virginia suddenly comes to be perceived as one of the best among the fifty states in being business-friendly. We will then experience a quantum leap forward.

For West Virginia to cross that threshold, a majority of its citizens and voters must be perceived as understanding how the incentives of capitalism work, and the importance of those incentives. Of course, many West Virginians already understand these things, but many do not. In order to help spread the word, it will not hurt for us to look quickly at some of the important milestones in the defense of capitalism, which I do in the next section.

Milestones In The Defense Of Capitalism

Adam Smith—the Invisible Hand. The "case for capitalism" received a huge boost when Adam Smith published *The Wealth of Nations* in 1776. Smith is most famous for saying that an "Invisible Hand" guides the private pursuit of self-interest on the part of competing individuals within a more or less free market toward the overall betterment of society. Resources are allocated, and products are produced, in the ways that are best for a society; overall levels of well-being increase. To use the language of incentives, we can say that, for Smith, an economic system that encourages the pursuit of rational self-interest via market competition contains the best incentives for bettering society overall.

Smith is making a comparative point: A free market system is better than alternatives, such as mercantilism as it existed in Smith's time, where the government controlled trade to a large extent by means of subsidies and tariffs. He is not saying that in every case the private pursuit of self-interest on the part of competing individuals contributes to the betterment of society, nor is he defending the pursuit of self-interest on moral grounds.

Smith wants us to look at the large picture from an economic perspective.

John Locke and J. S. Mill—the protection of basic rights. Adam Smith's defense of economic freedom is reinforced by the work of philosophers who defend the existence of basic moral rights, and in particular the work of John Locke from the seventeenth century and J. S. Mill from the nineteenth century. Locke's views regarding "natural rights" are the primary inspiration for the pronouncement in the American Declaration of Independence that human beings are endowed with "certain unalienable Rights, that among these are Life, Liberty and the pursuit of Happiness." For Locke, basic rights come from the fact that human beings are inherently equal and independent, which is to say that human beings are born with basic rights. In his *Two Treatises of Government*, published in 1689, Locke says that the basic human rights are life, liberty, and the ownership of property. Locke's defense of basic rights is not expressed in terms of incentives, but rather in terms of foundational moral values: Basic rights need to be protected simply because doing so is morally correct.

The protection of basic rights goes hand in hand with capitalism. From the perspective of someone who is morally committed to upholding basic rights, we can say that such a person possesses a strong internal incentive to uphold those rights. Historically, Locke has been understood to provide a defense for limited, capitalistic government that is separate from the type of defense that is linked to the creation of the best external economic incentives, such as those provided by Smith's Invisible Hand.

J. S. Mill in the 19th century defends basic rights in a way that is quite different from the approach taken by Locke. Mill argues that a society that possesses laws and traditions for the protection of basic rights will produce much higher levels of happiness for a greater number of people than will societies that do not have such laws and traditions. Thus, Mill's approach has a lot in common with Smith's approach: Both focus on structuring society in a way that benefits people the most. While rights for Mill are not inherent in human nature as they are for Locke, they are still extremely important because the protection of rights does so much, says Mill, toward bringing about the "greatest good for the greatest number." Mill's approach can easily be stated in terms of incentives: Laws and traditions protecting basic rights provide people with the best set of incentives for achieving the greatest good for members of society. Mill's views regarding rights are to be found especially in his *On Liberty*, published in 1859.

Regardless of whether one follows Locke or follows Mill in defending basic rights, the protection of rights is closely tied to capitalism. In order for a "right to liberty" to be meaningful, for example, people need to be able to own and control property—or at least money—in regard to business ventures, recreation, education, hobbies, supporting their families, or for any other goal within reason that they choose for themselves. The freedom to make choices goes hand in hand with having control over the means to act on those choices.

Friedrich Hayek—The "Spontaneous Order" of a free market. An important milestone in the defense of capitalism for the twentieth century was the publication of Friedrich Hayek's *The Road to Serfdom* in 1944. Hayek is most famous for arguing that capitalism is greatly superior to any planned, or government run, economy as regards both the quality and the quantity of information available to people who make business-related decisions. Capitalism is the most efficient economic system, with no close competitors, says Hayek. One of the main reasons is that capitalism is the best system for making crucial information available to the people who need it. The decisions made every day by buyers, sellers, manufacturers, suppliers, workers, investors, and others within a free market determine prices for goods, services, resources, facilities, labor, capital, and so on. These prices then serve an indispensable informational role for future business decisions, which in turn contribute to the information that is available for the next round of decisions. The result is a "spontaneous order" that is highly beneficial, and for which there exists no substitute. Prices are driven down, quality is improved, shortages of consumer goods are reduced or eliminated, resources and capital are most likely to be sent to the locations where they can best be used, workers are most likely to end up doing the jobs at which they excel or that society most needs to have done, and innovative technologies are most likely to be developed and utilized.

Hayek's spontaneous order is a bottom-up way to organize an economy, in contrast to the top-down approach of a planned, or government run, economy. For Hayek, the efficient use of resources absolutely requires the pricing mechanism of an essentially free market. The spontaneous order of a market economy can be thought of as comprising a vast, interlocking set of finely-tuned incentives for economic decision-makers at all levels. It is a set of incentives that cannot be duplicated in any other way.

By contrast, says Hayek, government planners can never come close to generating or possessing the quality and quantity of finely-tuned information that is available within a free market. The information possessed by government economic planners never comes close to being complete and is usually out of date. The more that government is involved in the economy, the more that essential information gets covered up; decisions are made in response to the wrong incentives. In addition, there is the problem that government planners are easily corrupted because of the strong political incentives that they face. These political incentives can hamper the operations of businesses that are constrained by government planning.

Joseph Schumpeter—"Creative Destruction." Another twentieth century milestone in the defense of capitalism was the publication in 1934 of Joseph Schumpeter's *The Theory of Economic Development*. In this book, Schumpeter writes about the importance of entrepreneurs in a free market economy—individuals who are willing to take risks, often very large risks, in introducing to the market new products, services, and ways of doing things. New products and services that prove to be successful are often at the expense of older products and services, which are removed from the market via a process of "creative destruction": Older and less efficient companies cease to exist or are scaled back, freeing up resources, facilities, and workers for newer ventures. The possibility that a company will face creative destruction if it is not successful provides a strong incentive for the people who run the company to do their best.

The highly beneficial aspects of creative destruction are sidetracked when government intervenes in the economy, and especially when it subsidizes or shelters from competition struggling or failing businesses that are not being run as well as they could be. If government is extensively involved in the economy of a state or country, its role is almost guaranteed to be counterproductive since politicians face strong incentives from special interest groups to prop up all of the struggling and failing older businesses in their districts that are facing strong competitive pressures from newer ventures. At the extreme are economically unsound companies judged to be "too large to fail," where government bailouts or takeovers interfere with creative destruction on an especially large scale. But creative destruction is absolutely required at all scales, Schumpeter says, in order for resources, capital, facilities, and skilled employees to be utilized in the most efficient ways, since all of these exist in limited quantities. Utilizing them in the best ways is critical for the strength of an economy.

The make-it-or-break-it difference between competitive success or failure for the economy of a state or a country often lies in the degree of creative destruction that is allowed or encouraged by the government of the state or country in question.

(I should mention here that my New Direction for Capitalism does allow for a special type of exception where "too large to fail" is sometimes an acceptable reason for government intervention—namely, as regards certain financial institutions that are closely linked to a national banking system such as the Federal Reserve. For NDC, this is the only permissible type of case where governmental intervention may be warranted for the purpose of preventing an institution from failing and dragging down the larger economy with it. The most recent example occurred in 2008-09 when the federal government via the Treasury Department and the Federal Reserve provided support to banks and other lending institutions. However, nothing else should ever be judged "too large to fail." No other types of large enterprises should be subsidized by government or sheltered from the creative destruction of the marketplace. I discuss these points further in Chapter 10.)

In the next chapter, I say more about why the American capitalistic ideal is in trouble at the present time.

Chapter 4.
Capitalism in Recessions and Depressions

As I mentioned in Chapter 2, one of the reasons why the American capitalistic ideal is in trouble at the present time is that too much blame is assigned to capitalism when an economic crisis occurs. I say more about this criticism of capitalism in the present chapter. Following that, I discuss where my New Direction for Capitalism fits in.

The Great Depression

In 1936, the economist John Maynard Keynes published his *General Theory of Employment, Interest and Money*, at a time when the Great Depression of the 1930s had been underway for several years. Critics of free market economics have always blamed the Great Depression on capitalism. Keynes offered a formula for government intervention in the economy that was supposed to end depressions by compensating for the alleged inadequacies of capitalism.

The important question, however, is the following. Was the Great Depression caused by activities in the private sector or instead by government interventions in the economy? It is unfair simply to assume that the free market portion of a mixed economy such as the United States has always possessed is the part that is to blame for serious problems.

For example, just prior to the Great Depression, policies of the Federal Reserve held interest rates below market levels, encouraging speculative investments at a time when market forces by themselves would have put a damper on those investments. The speculations got out of hand, people over-extended themselves, a lot of money was loaned for shaky enterprises. Following the stock market crash in 1929, the Federal Reserve pursued a tight money policy when it should have loosened credit instead; again, the people in charge made a bad mistake (but one that we can learn from). Then during the 1930s, the Roosevelt administration imposed additional restrictions on the market at home, and supported higher tariffs on imports that started a trade war with Europe and undermined American exports, thus destroying jobs. Add to all of this the fact that, by constantly readjusting his economic policies, President Roosevelt created a climate of uncertainty that scared off investors and undermined consumer confidence. Making the situation even worse was the fact that, in his frequent speeches to the American public, Roosevelt often expressed anticapitalist and anti-business sentiments; Roosevelt's speeches further undermined the confidence of business managers and investors. Finally, by following the advice of people who thought like Keynes, the federal government continually siphoned off capital from the private sector to spend on government programs intended to stimulate the economy and produce jobs. Many of these programs were wasteful and corrupt.

How corrupt? My father was a young man during the Roosevelt years, and told me stories about his experiences. He was employed for a time in the 1930s by the Works Progress

Administration, doing construction work on public projects. Much of what he did on the job was makeshift, and he was required to kick back to his boss a portion of his wages each week in order to keep his job. The boss himself did little actual work at the job site and very little overseeing of the work of employees. Eventually, the work crew did complete a worthwhile road construction project, but not efficiently and not honestly. The United States would have been much better off during the 1930s if its scarce capital had been used in better ways than this.

The Free Market View Of Recessions And Depressions

Free market economists predict that a capitalistic society will be subject to periodic recessions that function as a self-governing mechanism by which markets adjust themselves to an accumulation of unwise business decisions, natural disasters, the disruptive effects of technological change, and other factors. Recessions serve an essential informational function, enabling people at all levels within a market economy to better serve as genuine experts within the relatively narrow confines of their jobs as managers, sales staff, investors, bankers, and so on. Recessions help to ensure that economic incentives remain in tune with economic realities. Recessions need not be severe in order to serve this essential function.

A free market economy can be expected to go through phases where it grows more or less rapidly or even contracts for a period of time. But if it is left alone, it will straighten itself out, and will do so more quickly than if government intervenes, because better incentives will be in place. The likelihood that the recession will turn into a depression will be lessened. The interventionist "experts" tell a very different story, however.

According to Keynes in his *General Theory*, the best way to end a deep recession or a depression is for government to spend a lot of money. It does not matter that during a depression, because tax revenues go way down, government has little money to spend unless it goes further into debt, nor does it matter a great deal what the money is spent on. Roosevelt spent a lot of money during the 1930s, although not to much effect. Keynes' ideas even then scarcely made sense and had no meaningful support in practice—no genuine empirical support. But if an economic theory is to serve as the rationale for government interventions in the economy, it absolutely must be a well-tested theory.

Recent Events

In the fall of 2008 the United States experienced a severe economic downturn that soon came to affect numerous countries around the world, including countries that, like the United States, possess strong capitalistic elements, such as European countries, Japan, Australia, and Canada. The economic downturn affected less capitalistic countries as well, including Russia and China. The blame for the 2008 downturn was rightly placed more on the United States than on any other country since the main triggering event was the home mortgage crisis in the United States that began in 2008.

Many critics of capitalism say the following: The mortgage crisis occurred initially in the United States; the United States is a capitalistic country; therefore, the system of capitalism is to blame, or largely to blame, for the economic downturn of 2008. This view of the situation is unfair.

Defenders of capitalism place most of the blame for the economic downturn of 2008 on the *non-capitalistic elements* within the United States, such as the fact that the major lending institutions where most of the bad mortgages originated, namely Fannie Mae and Freddie Mac, belonged as much to government as they did to the private sector during the time when most of the bad loans were made. The federal government, going back to the time of the Clinton administration and continuing through the years of the succeeding Bush administration, strongly encouraged the granting of loans to individuals who failed to meet long-established criteria for being creditworthy. A lot of pressure was put on Fannie Mae and Freddie Mac. As added encouragement, long-established rules for the capitalization of banks were changed for Fannie Mae and Freddie Mac, allowing them to loan out more money in relation to their capital reserves than had previously been allowed; essentially, they were being urged to play a riskier lending game than previously in order to give out more mortgages to more people. The motive for all of this was political and moral, not economic or capitalistic in a strict sense, namely to enable a wider economic class of individuals to enjoy home ownership.

In addition, there has existed for some time in the United States an implicit understanding that the federal government would come to the aid of lending institutions that ended up with severe liquidity problems, especially if those institutions were large enough. The federal government did exactly this, for example, in response to the Savings and Loan crisis of the late 1980s and early 1990s. The fact that lending rules were changed for Fannie Mae and Freddie Mac, and that pressure was applied to them by the government to grant larger and larger numbers of mortgages, strengthened the implicit understanding that the federal government would come to their aid if there were problems.

Lastly, during the years when most of the bad loans were

being made by Fannie Mae and Freddie Mac, the Federal Reserve kept interest rates too low for too long as a mistaken response to the dot-com market collapse in 2001-02. Borrowing money had never been easier.

In short, prior to 2008 the federal government created strong incentives for banks to grant loans to individuals who, from a purely business perspective, would never have been granted the loans, and banks were also given strong incentives to grant loans in larger numbers than prudent business practices would have dictated even if the loans in themselves had not carried any additional risk. At the same time, the existence of unusually low interest rates further strengthened incentives for unqualified buyers and speculators to purchase homes and other real estate. With all of these people buying homes, home prices were bound to rise, which provided even stronger incentives for speculators to enter the real estate market in the hope of making quick profits by buying and then re-selling houses. Of course, this situation could not be sustained indefinitely. Initial small drops in home prices for some housing markets triggered the collapse. By keeping interest rates too low in the years prior to 2008, and by pressuring banks to make loans to unqualified buyers, the federal government had stopped vital information from flowing to the people who most needed this information. It had become more difficult in the years immediately preceding 2008 for bankers and others to appreciate the extent to which people buying houses and other real estate were overextending themselves.

Not surprisingly, critics of capitalism tell a wholly different story. They argue that the 2008 economic downturn would not have occurred if numerous lending institutions and investment firms had not taken unfair advantage of the situation in two different ways: First, by encouraging people

with high incomes as well as low incomes, and also speculators, to take out mortgages even though these people failed
to meet standard criteria for being credit-worthy; second, by
repackaging and selling substandard mortgages as investments (Mortgage Based Securities, often referred to as MBS)
that, according to the story told at the time by the banks that
sold them, would yield large returns and were safe for the
future. However, while many MBS did yield significant short
term gains, insufficient attention was paid to the prospects for
long term losses on the part of both sellers and buyers of these
investments, especially as regards variable rate mortgages.
Likewise, numerous banks promoted mortgages to rich and
poor alike in a morally reprehensible fashion by emphasizing
the immediate attraction of initial low payments on variable
rate mortgages while downplaying the large risks to buyers
for the future, when interest rates would almost surely esca-
late (but the banks did not usually mention this), and when
the prices for homes might drop. In other words, according to
the critics of capitalism, financial incentives that were put in
place by the federal government in order to help low income
families and minorities were abused by "greedy capitalists"
who wanted to make a fast buck. These individuals did not
possess the right sorts of moral incentives, nor were their activities properly regulated by the federal government because
of its bias toward free market ideas.

Each Side Is Partly Right

The position taken in this book is that each side to the debate about what caused the 2008 mortgage crisis is partly on
the right track. It is true both that *departures* from capitalism
played an important role and also that the reprehensible and
shortsighted way in which numerous individuals *within* the

capitalistic system sought to make profits played an important role. The 2008 mortgage crisis would not have occurred if the sorts of governmental interventions and mistakes described above had not occurred. But it is also true that the 2008 mortgage crisis would not have been as severe as it was if the major players in the private sector had taken the moral high road.

The debate regarding the 2008 mortgage crisis can be broadened to include capitalism as a whole. Again, each side to the more general debate is partly right. On the one hand, the present American economic system needs to be improved by making it more capitalistic, indeed much more capitalistic. It is crucial that incentives belonging to market competition be strengthened a great deal within West Virginia, the United States as a whole, and other countries. The protection of property rights needs to be strengthened in West Virginia and elsewhere. Taxes and red tape need to be reduced very substantially. Supporters of capitalism who complain that today's capitalistic societies are all being dragged down by the presence of strong non-capitalistic economic elements in these societies are essentially correct. What we have is not capitalism, but semi-capitalism. We have a mixed economy. Unquestionably, there is a great need for economic reforms that will move us in a capitalistic direction. A window of opportunity exists at the present time for West Virginia to take a strong lead in these reforms, and become a much more prosperous state and an all-around better place to live.

On the other hand, and equally important, numerous individuals within the United States and other capitalistic, or semi-capitalistic, societies need to think very differently from a moral perspective than they do at the present time about the way in which profits are to be made. Much more attention should be paid to the prospects for long-term benefits to companies, consumers, taxpayers, and society at large. An attitude of "take the money and run" must be discouraged by everyone. In short, moral advancement is needed just as much as economic advancement, and this is true for all of the world's capitalistic societies (and its few remaining wholly non-capitalistic societies as well—but the story takes some different turns for them). Each type of advancement that I have just mentioned is incomplete without the other. A window of opportunity exists for West Virginia to take a strong lead as regards both types of advancement. It is an opportunity for our state to make good on the slogan **Low Taxes, Least Red Tape, Highest Ethics**.

When the two types of advancement are combined in the right way, the result is my New Direction for Capitalism. NDC is not strict laissez-faire capitalism, as I have indicated. For NDC, government must play a role in helping people in need and making society a better place overall, but this role must be properly restricted in order not to undermine the main benefits of capitalism.

Capitalism when properly understood really is as good as Adam Smith, Friedrich Hayek, Henry Hazlitt, Milton Friedman, and others have said that it is, but it is good only as an *economic system* that needs to be supplemented by an improved *moral outlook*. What is needed is NDC. The type of limited government prescribed by NDC provides freedom and security under the law, while also providing maximum opportunities for people to try out various ways to organize communities, run charities, strengthen friendships, and develop businesses that provide worthwhile products and services. NDC-guided government accomplishes all of this while allowing for the imperfections of human nature, human knowledge, and human intentions.

How Do We Make It Happen?

Of course, readers will have questions about my New Direction for Capitalism, and about how it applies to West Virginia and to the United States as a whole. By the end of this book, I hope to have given satisfactory answers to all of your questions. You may be thinking that one question stands out at this point, and that I need to begin to answer it here, namely the question of implementation for the moral half of NDC: How does a society get people to behave more morally within a largely free market economy? This is indeed a important question. It may seem, as well, to be an especially difficult question to answer.

By contrast, the *free market* half of NDC is straightforward. People simply respond to the incentives of the marketplace once they are in place. To the extent that capitalism exists, these incentives exist; and capitalism can be made to exist by legislation that establishes the right kind of limited government that supports economic freedom and business competition. All that is required is the will of the people at election times. But the moral half of NDC is quite different because "you cannot legislate morality," at least not easily or extensively. Yet, people disregard moral values all the time, as the 2008 economic crisis vividly demonstrates. Therefore, what choice is there except to have government force people to behave as they should by placing more, not fewer, restrictions on their economic activities than presently exist? Should we not be *moving away* from capitalism rather than toward it? Isn't this the best response to the 2008 economic crisis? Numerous critics of capitalism at the present time argue along these lines.

My reply is that the same "will of the people" that can and should move the state of West Virginia and the country as a whole toward free market reforms at election times can and should push the state and the country *at all times* toward greater levels of moral behavior in the domains of business and politics. Earlier, I said that no country or state will enjoy a strong economy for long if its voters are not perceived as possessing a sufficient understanding of capitalism, since otherwise there is no assurance that capitalistic reforms that are passed today will not be repealed tomorrow—and investors know this all too well. Now I am saying that for economic reforms to work most effectively there must also exist the perception that large numbers of people in a country or a state will express their displeasure *just as much* when there are moral failures on the part of business or government as when there are economic failures.

The fact is that West Virginia, the United States, and the world at large are now at a crossroads where the make-it-or-break-it difference between success and failure in the years ahead lies in the understanding and will of voters and citizens. As I see it, there can exist no stronger force for good on the face of the planet than an informed citizenry as regards what I wish to describe as the two halves of my New Direction for Capitalism—the economic half and the moral half. To be properly informed, people must not depend only on the pronouncements of politicians, mainstream media outlets, and other popular sources of information. This book is an unabashed attempt to steer the understanding of voters and citizens in what I believe to be the right direction.

I say a lot more in later chapters by way of answering the question of what can be done to make both the economic half and the moral half of NDC work.

I turn now to a serious problem that arises in all capitalistic countries like the United States. It is a problem that is closely connected to understanding the causes for recessions and depressions.

A Lethal Combination

As virtually everyone knows, the United States and numerous other countries are not examples of pure capitalism but instead are examples of mixed economies that contain both capitalistic and non-capitalistic elements. The sad fact is that, in the absence of sufficiently large numbers of informed voters, mixed economies are not stable. They contain the seeds for their own destruction, and this is all the more true when the defense of capitalism is linked to the egoism of Ayn Rand or the pure profit-seeking model for business of Milton Friedman, which I discussed earlier. When the type of mixed economy possessed by the United States at the present time is combined with the pure profit-seeking model, for example, a lethal combination results. On the one hand, people are effectively told to go all out to make money in business. (This is not exactly what Friedman says in *Capitalism and Freedom* and elsewhere, but it is easy to get the impression that this is what he says.) On the other hand, today's federal and state governments are heavily involved in the world of business, ready to provide favors to whoever will give candidates the most support at election times. The result is that business people can often increase their companies' profits the most by doing things that undermine capitalism rather than strengthen it. The following is a partial list of the favors that businesses can, and do, ask government to provide:

* Tax breaks, or tax incentives, for themselves at the expense of competitors
* Tariffs and other trade restrictions that reduce competition
* Funding (earmarks) for projects that favor one's own business or industry

* Licensing requirements that favor already established businesses at the expense of new competition
* Environmental laws that favor one industry over another
* Labor laws, executive decisions, and financial regulations that favor one industry over another, or one business over another
* The exercise of eminent domain on behalf of one's own business and against the interests of competitors
* Low interest government loans that favor one's own business
* Special treatment in leasing or buying land or resources from the government
* Antimonopoly laws or decisions that hurt one's competitors more than oneself
* Bailout money that is not distributed impartially
* Favorable judicial decisions
* Favorable treatment in receiving government contracts

In short, within the type of mixed economy possessed by the United States—and to a greater or lesser extent by most countries around the world at the present time—people in business are confronted by strong incentives to "game the system" rather than simply to do their best to provide goods and services at the best prices. The more that gaming of the system takes place, the worse the overall situation becomes: Business people become accustomed to "going to the government" when they have problems rather than trying to solve their problems on their own within a free market. Lobbying skills become more important than management skills. Large amounts of money are given by corporations, trade unions, trade organizations, professional groups, etc., to support lobbying efforts and to influence the outcomes of elections. But the more that elections are influenced by special interests, the more that people in government become dependent upon financial support from business lobbyists and others, and thus the more that people in government come to possess strong incentives to create new opportunities for businesses—and everyone else—to game the system. The problems that belong to this collusive business/government system feed upon themselves and grow at an accelerating pace. Economic instability increases. The likelihood that a country will experience a severe recession or depression increases.

So, as I said, the type of mixed economy possessed by the United States and numerous other countries contains the seeds for its own destruction. It is not surprising that critics of capitalism emphasize the need for "greedy capitalists" to clean up their act, or else for government to regulate them even more strictly or take them over altogether. From the perspective of NDC, there is a great deal of merit to the charge that business people should clean up their act, and especially that they should back away from their efforts to succeed in business by buying the support of people in government. Certainly, the idea that it is OK "from the perspective of capitalism" to take any action that is legal in an effort to make money in business is totally objectionable. However, the main point that I want to make regarding the lethal combination of a mixed economy and the pure profit-seeking model is that the *economic incentives for corruption* within a mixed economy such as the U.S. presently possesses are so strong that they absolutely must be changed in a free market direction, in conjunction with improvements in the moral consciousness of numerous business people and politicians.

In other words, true reform requires my New Direction for Capitalism, or something like it, both within West Virginia and the U.S. as a whole. In the next chapter, I say more about how economics and morality fit together within NDC.

Chapter 5.
The Ideal of Limited Government

At the heart of my New Direction for Capitalism is the concept of an "informed consenting adult"—someone who examines a number of options, gathers information about them, and then decides which to follow. As much as possible, government does not limit the number of options. This restriction on government's role applies to most spheres of life: religion, business, education, medicine, science, art, entertainment, charity, finding meaning in life. It is the immensely important negative requirement for limited government, namely, to intrude as little as possible into people's lives—to leave people alone. The main positive requirement (the main job that government absolutely must do), which is just as important, is for government to ensure that people leave each other alone—to increase to the maximum the protection given to everyone in making their choices in life and holding onto their lives, health, freedom, property, and happiness.

In today's world, the protective function of government is becoming more difficult every day because of the ease with which rogue nations and terrorists can use sophisticated weapons and advanced technologies for destructive purposes. Even common criminals can possess automatic pistols, assault rifles, bombs, and worse. Criminals and terrorists from many different backgrounds have access to advanced technologies for communication, travel, hiding assets, transporting weapons, and concealing identities. Dense populations in big cities are especially vulnerable to terrorism and sabotage, and the same is true of passengers packed together in an airliner. Simultaneously, criminals and terrorists are becoming much more skillful at stealing money, information, and people's identities via computers and electronic surveillance. New methods of counterfeiting currency are constantly being developed.

The answer to all of this is to remove government from areas where it does not belong so that it can concentrate on doing the jobs that it must do. Essential jobs include not only protecting us from criminals and terrorists at home and abroad but also protecting us from businesses at home and abroad whose activities may jeopardize our well-being—power plants that pollute the air, oil companies that allow oil spills, pharmaceutical companies that produce harmful drugs, and indeed any human activities where solid scientific evidence shows that substantial harm will result. In the private sector, successful enterprises are ones that specialize and find their niche. Governments must do likewise. They must learn to specialize much more than at present in order to do their jobs properly. The concept of governmental specialization is central to my New Direction for Capitalism.

At the furthest extreme from NDC is totalitarian government. Life under a dictator, benevolent or otherwise, exists within a single "level of organization" that consists of the decrees of the ruler. Not only must the dictator run the country, but this same individual must also continually tinker with the fundamental system for ruling—playing off one advisor against another, strengthening the military against the judiciary, weakening the military against business leaders, promising an election but finding an excuse not to hold it. Necessarily, the dictator will have little time to address the country's problems even if the dictator is genuinely interested in solving those problems.

The President of the Unites States is immeasurably better off because the President's relations with Congress, the Cabinet, and the court system are essentially stable. Still, the President under our existing form of government is expected to understand nearly all spheres of life *and* master the complexities of dealing with Congress, the public, news media, and foreign governments. Members of Congress, likewise, are expected to possess a superhuman breadth of understanding. The U.S. government is expected to be all things to all people. The result is hugely problematic.

A Huge Dilemma

If government policies are resistant to change, as most are, then improving the way things are done (in business, education, medicine, you name it) is difficult. But if government policies can be changed easily, then people have incentives to use government for their own immediate advantage rather than to make it a better system overall. People have incentives to change government in the wrong direction, which is what is happening at the present time in an increasing number of different areas. Only NDC, or something close to it, escapes from the horns of this dilemma.

As an illustration, if government runs all of the schools and the schools are not doing a good job, then for education to be improved, changes must take place at both the level of government *and* within the schools—a huge job that will take a long time if it can be accomplished at all. And if it is accomplished, it will likely be on behalf of whichever interest group has the most effective lobbyists. By contrast, if more of the schools are run privately or separately, which can be accomplished by having charter schools or a voucher system for education, we must change only the schools. Moreover, we can begin right here with our own school or we can build a new school. We are not obligated to reform the entire educational system, not to mention the underlying governmental system, in order to start the ball rolling toward innovation and improvement. The incentives that we face can motivate us quickly to achieve valuable reforms, especially since the reforms will initially be local and on a small scale, and will be subject to actual or potential competition. If we do not get the reforms right the first time, we can try again before a lot of time has passed.

Many people cannot afford high quality schooling for their children, which is one reason why government must play a substantial role. There is nothing wrong with having government pay, or help to pay, for education. Problems lie with the various roles that government must play when it actually runs all, or most, of the schools. If government does run some of the schools, which is to be expected in today's world, and which does have benefits, then if there also exist avenues for opening charter schools or for implementing a voucher system, public schools will face possible competition, and this situation will work toward the betterment of all schools. Where public schools *are* doing a good job, which is certainly true for some West Virginia cities and towns, there will be no need for anyone to actually make use of the charter or voucher option, but having such options available in the background will still be important.

Having a voucher or charter option available introduces the beneficial incentives that come into existence when there is competition. A single school, whether public or private, that is genuinely better within a more or less free market for education will "force" other schools to imitate its success, because that is the nature of competition. Likewise, a single hospital that offers better health care at a good price within a more or less free market will force other hospitals to imitate its success. Here too, there is nothing wrong with having government help to pay for medical care for people who cannot do so themselves, as long as government does not run the health care system—and as long as there exist effective incentives for people who do receive help from the government to work toward a time when, if possible, they can themselves pay for more of their own health care. The same reasoning applies in other areas of life as well.

In today's global economy, talented and hardworking people whose skills or capital are in demand naturally gravitate toward countries that have good schools and hospitals, along with other benefits, thus putting pressure on other countries to improve in all of these areas as well. The same is true regarding states and provinces within countries: Whenever they have opportunities to do so, people and businesses will move to the best locations. Owners of businesses will reduce or close down their operations in one state, and reopen or expand in another state. Needless to say, we want West Virginia to be the state that comes out on top when this occurs. Investments will flow to the best locations, namely the ones where governments foster the existence of the best sorts of incentives for health care, education, business, protecting the environment, fairness in the judicial system, and everything else. (Of course, we want West Virginia to be the best location of all!)

In most domains of life, we are in much better shape if government limits its role on the "playing field of life" while simultaneously fulfilling all of its essential roles in the background of our lives.

This is true even if a particular governmental agency is likely to make a wise decision in an individual case. In fact, it is easy to imagine numerous situations where we might be tempted to call upon government to expand its role in our lives. Nothing is more natural than for someone to say even in the best of situations: "I know a way to make things even better," or to say in a less happy situation: "I know a way to straighten out this mess." The next thing said will be: "Give me the authority to fix the situation and I will solve your problems. Even better, make me the ruler so that I can marshal resources from across the entire country in order to solve problems in the best way." Thus is born the main rationale for a wide range of governmental interventions in human affairs. When the interventions are partial, the result is a mixed economy such as presently exists in the U.S. and most other countries. (When the interventions are total or nearly so, the result is socialism, where government runs virtually everything—and runs it straight into the ground.)

I am not saying that the mixed economy model is wrong. The position defended in this book is that for government to work well the mixture must *strongly favor* private sector over public sector contributions within the context of a mixed economy. From where we are at the present time, we need to move in a capitalistic direction in order to arrive at the proper mixture.

The Corrupting Effect Of Big Government

Big governments tend to bring out the worst in nearly everyone. Bullies and tyrants are attracted to governmental power because they enjoy pushing people around. Unscrupulous corporate leaders find that buying favors from government is second nature, and the success of their efforts under a governmental system such as the U.S. presently possesses gives them incentives to increase their efforts. Ambulance chasing lawyers delight in the spaghetti of laws, codes, and government regulations that give them work. Decent, moral, hard-working individuals employed by government cannot always resist powerful incentives to say and do what is politically expedient in order to advance their careers, or simply to save their jobs, as opposed to what these individuals may believe is right and true—or may once have believed was right and true, before their beliefs were corrupted by the system of which they are a part.

Observing all this, many people are inclined to say: "That's just the way the world is." But they're wrong. It's the way the world is *under big government.* And there is more to the story when we consider further the interplay between big government and large corporations.

Economies of scale are at work that make coping with big government much easier for large corporations than for small businesses or for individuals. Large corporations have a better chance to become strong competitors because of these economies of scale. However, this phenomenon cuts both ways, and some of the consequences are extremely detrimental to the well-being of society as a whole: Big companies can deal more easily with big government in cutting through red tape to provide needed goods and services (and this is a good thing), but big companies are also likely to be corrupted in coming to rely on government in order to be successful. On the one hand, large companies have an unfair advantage over smaller companies or newly founded companies in regard to how easily any of these companies can master the complexities of government regulations and tax codes in order to operate efficiently. On the other hand, large companies can easily be induced to backslide in terms of how efficiently they are run and how well they meet consumers' needs, once they get into the habit of accepting favors from government rather than putting their own house in order.

A company that grosses many millions of dollars in sales can employ its own in-house tax attorneys, lobbyists, and professional analysts of governmental policies. It can use its expertise in dealing with government as a wedge against competitors. Likewise, the "revolving door" between governmental and corporate employment benefits the rich and powerful much more than anyone else because the rich and powerful are better placed, first, to obtain influential government jobs, and second, to make use of their influence with government officials once they return to the private sector. At election times, individuals who are rich and powerful can actually make their presence known by hobnobbing with senators and the president at five-thousand-dollars-a-plate dinners, while people who send in their twenty dollar campaign donations are lucky to see their candidates at a whistle stop.

For government to benefit the very rich by means of interventions in the economy, all it needs to do is give them an unfair advantage over everyone else, which is easy to accomplish because the very rich constitute a small minority of the population. They can be given substantial tax breaks, generous government contracts, large government subsidies, lucrative employment via the revolving door between government and industry, and other kinds of help. By contrast, the number of people who are not rich is much too large for any such attempts at favoritism to be effective. Likewise, the number of small companies across the country is much too large for attempts at favoritism to have much effect. It is impossible for government to give lucrative contracts to large numbers of people in the middle class, nor does government have enough money to give low interest loans to every small business.

Programs intended to help large companies and individuals who are rich and powerful are likely to pay off here and now, which gives these companies and these individuals strong incentives to support the politicians who are on their side. Programs intended to benefit the middle and lower economic classes are more in the nature of vague, long-term promises, which means that their failure to be fulfilled can eventually be blamed on someone other than the politicians who originally made the promises at election time.

Corporate Collectivism

Michael Harrington, who until his death in 1989 was the best known American advocate of socialism, was fond of saying that the economic system under which we live in the United States is not capitalism but "corporate collectivism." Big business and big government collude for mutual benefit, he said. The government of the United States uses its extensive powers of intervention primarily on behalf of existing big businesses and wealthy individuals, putting small businesses and people in the middle and lower classes at a disadvantage. Harrington's solution was to make the U.S. government "more responsive to the people" by transforming it into a type of democratic socialism. A much better solution is to reduce the scope of government, preferably on the model of NDC.

There is only one good way to control the incentives built into government which favor the rich and the powerful, and that is to minimize the extent to which government can play favorites with anyone.

Please notice that what I have just said does not presuppose any particular view of human nature. Critics of capitalism have long maintained that capitalism as a social system appeals essentially to human selfishness and greed, which, they say, is one of the reasons why we should expect that there will be extensive collusion between government and big business. But this is not the correct way to look at the situation. Properly understood, capitalism does not "see the human race" any way at all. Rather, it provides the best system of incentives for dealing with people of all types, good, bad, and indifferent. If human beings *were* mostly selfish and greedy, then capitalistic government along the lines of NDC would be the best political and economic system because it would minimize opportunities and incentives for collusion between government and business. But just as much, if human beings were all saints, capitalistic government along the lines of NDC would still be the best, because even saints can disagree as to what constitutes the most saintly course of action, and one group of saints would likely call upon government to help *them*, at the expense of another group of saints, if the opportunity were there. Besides, if government is given a great deal of power, how can we distinguish in every case between saints and "benevolent despots"? The truth is that saints and sinners alike can benefit from the freedoms and protections afforded by free market economics and politics.

Capitalistic government along the lines of NDC is the best type of government in a world that contains some true saints, some wholly greedy and selfish people, and large numbers who fall somewhere in between.

Helping People In Need, Promoting The General Welfare

For NDC, government should play limited roles as regards helping people in need, as I said above. These roles are, however, extremely important. Because of the nature of the incentives necessarily built into the way that government operates, such strictly limited roles are the only ones that government can handle effectively without becoming corrupted itself or exercising a corrupting influence on people and businesses. The bottom line is that governments are not good at running things, especially when there is no competition apart from what the government is doing. Sometimes we have no choice but to allow the government to run something with no outside competition—the military is a good example—but the lesson to take home here is the importance of minimizing the areas where government ends up running things and being completely in charge.

Stopping things from happening. What governments are good at for a wide range of situations is stopping bad things from happening. National parks are an excellent example. The federal government has played an immensely valuable role in stopping many different American wilderness areas from being developed. In most cases, the government had only a one-shot opportunity to preserve a particular wilderness area, and for the obvious reason that wilderness, once it is gone, stays gone, at least in its original form. By contrast, the federal government has done only a so-so job of running national parks as tourist attractions.

The federal government has done an absolutely abysmal job in administering Social Security, or perhaps it would be better to say that the federal government has flat-out not administered Social Security—certainly not as a program for putting aside people's money to be used for retirement. Instead, the federal government has spent the money raised from Social Security taxes, while leaving future benefits to be paid out of future revenues. As everyone knows by now, there is no real money in the so-called Social Security Trust Fund, which is nothing more than an accounting device for reporting the total difference between income and outgo for Social Security for past years up to the present. When stated as a dollar amount, this difference is something like two and one half trillion dollars at the present time, which looks good on paper; but it exists only in the form of IOUs from the U.S. Treasury. The sad fact is that incentives within our present political system have proven to be too much for the typical politician, including the large number who have participated in emptying the Social Security Trust Fund of any real assets. In place of even attempting to administer Social Security as a program for putting aside people's money for retirement, politicians have instead spent the money in their efforts to "please the voters" (and advance their own careers) at election times.

Should government play any role at all regarding retirement benefits for Americans?

The properly negative role of government regarding Social Security. For NDC, the proper role of government regarding retirement benefits is essentially and primarily negative—stopping people from spending all of their own money much too soon. In other words, this is an area where government can effectively stop something bad from happening. Government has a special knack for doing this, as I said. Government can require people to set aside money for retirement, while also requiring that the money be entrusted to the private sector for actual investment. People can be directed to types of investment plans that meet certain basic requirements, such as adherence to a more conservative investment strategy as a person gets older, and government can provide a floor, or safety net, in the event that a person's retirement investments taken all together as a package fall substantially short of expectations, in order to ensure that retirement benefits are not wholly at the "mercy of the market." The only people whom government should routinely support in retirement out of general revenues are those who have not been able to put aside money of their own earlier in their lives, because of disability or severe misfortune.

The way to introduce a retirement plan such as I am describing here is slowly, through several phases, in order not to jeopardize the benefits to which people are entitled under the present Social Security system. The best place to start is probably to allow people under a certain age—people who are not yet retired or close to retirement—to split their yearly Social Security taxes between contributions to the present system and contributions to private investment, or to opt completely for the new system if this is what they prefer. Making the system voluntary in this way would create positive incentives of the best kind: Once a significant number of people have opted for the new system, and are pleased by the results in terms of the assets that they are accumulating, many other people will doubtless become motivated to join in.

One of the really neat things about a retirement program of the type that I am advocating here is that, except in a very general sense, no one in government needs to become an expert as regards exactly how people ought to invest their savings for retirement. No one in government needs to be an economic planner in any sort of comprehensive way. Instead, government's job is primarily to get people to invest for retirement by putting in place a strong negative external incentive: Requiring people to set aside an appropriate portion of their income or face a penalty. Individuals themselves can then become experts regarding the relatively narrow question of how to invest their own money. People are always much better motivated to look after their own money properly than to look after someone else's money. If government attempts to manage people's money, it will be subject to numerous corrupting incentives. It will not possess adequate motivation to engage the services of genuine experts in the field of money management, and it will not be free from powerful political incentives to divert the money to other uses.

In the next chapter, I say more about private sector/public sector access to the services of experts. I explain why the private sector has a huge advantage over the public sector where experts are concerned. But first I will answer the following question.

Why Should Government Be Involved At All?

Some readers may be wondering: Why should government require people to put money aside for retirement? Is this not an improper intrusion into our lives? Why should government play any role at all? Why can't we be allowed to make our own decisions as to how much money we will put aside for our own retirement?

Here is why government should play a role: If the motivation for saving for one's retirement is left entirely to the inner incentives of people themselves, a lot can and will go wrong. The number of people who do not possess the necessary incentives to save enough money is simply too large. In all likelihood, a significant number of people would reach retirement age without having accumulated sufficient savings, or any savings at all, toward supporting themselves in retirement, and then society would face the problem of how to care for these people. Government would need to be more actively involved in people's lives than it ought to be. Ideally, a person's rational assessment when young of what their needs will be when they are old will constitute a sufficient incentive to get them to put aside enough money for retirement. For many people, this is sufficient, but for many others it is not sufficient. The main problem is that strong incentives for spending money intervene along the way in the lives of many people that can seem at the time more important than one's far-off retirement—serious illnesses, children's needs, unemployment, failed businesses, bad luck, or the temptation to use a credit card to go on an expensive vacation that is beyond one's means. There is also the problem that some people may not possess a sufficiently strong sense of moral responsibility when young or middle-aged to take the steps needed in order not to be a burden on others when they are old.

Perhaps human nature could be changed through education and discipline so as to lessen these problems. But if this could be done easily, there would be more evidence that progress was being made. As for the future, it's hard to say what is feasible when it comes to changing people's outlook on life in any substantial way. In the meantime, it is clear that if we add a strong external incentive—a penalty for people who do not pay into a retirement fund—we will get good results. Once people reach retirement age, most of them will be happy that they were required earlier in life to save money systematically over the years. For the relatively small numbers of people who have not been able to earn enough during the course of their lives to be able to put money aside, because of disabilities or sheer bad luck, government can help out with subsidies. Government can also help out, as I mentioned above, if a person's retirement benefits—perhaps again as the result of bad luck, this time in making investments—fall below a certain minimal value.

A similar approach can be taken regarding health care: Have government require that people put money aside in medical savings accounts or as premiums for health insurance; have government subsidize health care for the poor and disabled; but see to it that government does not actually run any health care programs, except in the very limited context of case management by social workers employed by government for people receiving welfare support who have no health insurance. For health care just as for retirement benefits, the best solution is for government not to be in charge. I say more about health care in later chapters.

NDC—A Realistic Ideal For Today's World

Let me say first that not everyone in today's world favors the mixed economy model. For example, socialists do not favor it, but their numbers have declined greatly over the last half century. Socialists want to decrease the amount of freedom in the marketplace until it is nearly nonexistent, believing as they do that government control of the economy should replace virtually all market mechanisms. For socialists, government's "experts" should control most aspects of a country's economy. History has not been kind to socialism, nor does it fare any better from the perspective of economic theory. In truth, socialism places absolutely ludicrous demands on so-called experts in government, and also grossly underestimates the corrupting effects of concentrated power when it is exercised by government regardless of the levels of expertise actually possessed by the individuals who may be attempting to govern effectively. All in all, socialism generates extremely counterproductive economic and moral incentives.

A second example of those who reject the mixed economy model consists of libertarians, who assign only one moral role to government, namely the protection of basic rights, along with the economic freedom that is essential for the existence of basic rights. Although my New Direction for Capitalism has a lot in common with libertarianism, and certainly is much closer to libertarianism than to socialism, nevertheless NDC needs to be sharply distinguished from libertarianism. For NDC, government should play additional roles in promoting the overall good of society and helping people in need. NDC recognizes that the U.S. Constitution does not treat basic rights as absolute: The Constitution allows private property to be taken for public uses such as road-building, as long as there is just compensation as specified in the Fifth Amendment. NDC recognizes as well the framers' intention to "promote the general Welfare" that is mentioned in the Preamble to the Constitution.

The framers of the Constitution believed that government should play only a highly restricted role in promoting the overall good of society. Libertarians want to shrink this role even further. For libertarians, governments should mostly focus on the protective functions of government—police, military, courts, and (for some libertarians) supporting a strong currency. It's not that libertarians are necessarily opposed to the existence or exercise of moral goodwill, but rather that libertarians tend to see goodwill as being optional, at least as regards the functions of an ideal government or social system. Some libertarians do say that helping others is praiseworthy, but they do not say that it is praiseworthy in the way that the protection of freedom and basic rights is praiseworthy. For most libertarians, helping others for their own sake is not a strong, basic, essential moral value.

NDC emphatically rejects the libertarian view of morality and government to which I have just referred. Nevertheless, I believe that we can learn a lot from studying the writings of libertarians. NDC is not libertarianism, but it is closer to libertarianism than are most other views of government being defended at the present time. One of the main differences, as I have said, is that NDC government, unlike libertarian government, has a place for government-funded welfare for people in need across all age groups. Government also plays a role in guaranteeing that everyone has health care, education, and a pension in retirement. For NDC, government plays a role as well regarding such well-established institutions as national parks. Government properly exercises the power of eminent domain—in order to further the common good—as specified in the U.S. Constitution. Government plays additional important roles regarding the protection of the environment, public health, consumer safety issues, trade issues, and some others. For NDC as regards all functions of government, the goal is for government to put in place incentives that actually work, that do not undermine a strong economy, and that overall strengthen the protection of basic rights. For NDC, the roles of governmental experts are kept as narrowly prescribed and limited as possible in order to ensure that purported governmental experts really are experts (or come close to being experts) within the narrowed down confines of their jobs.

Whenever possible, government under NDC *provides money* for what is needed and places restrictions on how the money can be spent, but keeps to a minimum the *administration of programs* where the money is spent. Likewise, government requires people to invest on their own behalf, if they can, in support of retirement benefits, but allows the institutions of the market to handle the way that money is invested. Government requires that people put aside money for health care or health care insurance, if they can, but does not run any health care systems or medical insurance programs. Government stops people from despoiling wilderness areas or polluting the air or water, or creating environmental hazards, but adopts market mechanisms whenever possible to ensure that such protective goals of government are fulfilled in the most efficient ways.

NDC pays close attention to what motivational psychology tells us about how incentives actually work in the everyday world. Supporters of NDC want *effective* welfare programs, pension programs, universal health coverage, safety legislation, environmental legislation, trade agreements, and the rest.

NDC has the potential for uniting people in West Virginia, and in the United States as a whole, in the pursuit of goals that most people can agree on. NDC is a realistic ideal for today's world.

Chapter 6.
Public/Private Roles of Experts

In this Chapter I discuss what I call the "problem of placing experts in government." How do we ensure that people in policymaking positions in government possess the expertise required of them if they are to do their jobs properly? As an illustration of the seriousness of this problem, let us look first at government farm policies.

The federal government in the United States currently has in place a farm policy that includes tariffs, subsidies, price supports, tax credits, and other interventions. This policy has much in common with the farm policies that exist in a number of other democratic countries around the world. The voters in all of these countries elect the public officials who decide what the specifics of their country's farm policy will be. This naturally raises the following question: Do voters know enough to be entrusted with such a large responsibility? Farming, after all, is a highly complex business in itself, and farm policies have ramifications for numerous areas of life beyond farming.

Will Government Contain
The Experts Who Are Needed?

Let us imagine the following scenario: First, a majority of voters in a particular state learn enough about farming to be able to select the candidate who has the best ideas on the subject. In addition, these voters overcome all of the pressures that they face to vote on some other basis, with the result that the best "farm senator" gets elected. Then this senator studies farming day and night and becomes the world's top expert.

If all of these events came to pass, would they ensure that at least one senator knew what he/she was doing when the next Congressional Farm Bill came up for a vote?

The answer is *no*. The senator in question would not possess the required expertise.

Why not?

The job of the federal government is to do the best for farming *in relation to all other areas under its jurisdiction*. Government's job is to be fair and consistent in passing laws and enforcing laws. Government must find the right balance while doing what is best on behalf of everyone in the country. For a member of Congress to be a genuine expert on farming would be unusual enough. It is impossible for this same individual to be an expert as well in regard to energy, education, welfare, medical care, mail delivery, space exploration, forest management, trade, banking, national security, and numerous other areas where the federal government plays a large role in today's world. How can a senator be impartial when he or she is at best an expert in only one or a few of the areas across which impartiality is needed?

When a bill is up for a vote in Congress, what the contest usually comes down to is a question of which side has the greatest political strength—the side of those who are "pro-farming," the side of those who are "pro-consumer," the side of those who are "pro-industry," or the side of some other interest group. Few members of Congress can honestly say that they are impartial, and few would even want to *claim* that they are impartial at election times when they are seeking support from a specific group of constituents. Most politicians believe that the way to win an election is to appeal to a large enough set of sizable voting blocks, or interest groups. This means that Congress is essentially a battleground for clashing interest groups. Even to call some senators pro-farming is misleading because what the senators must do in order to stay in office is please the farming interests in their state—or the farmers in their state who donate to their campaigns—not farming as a whole across the country. Thus, senators are strongly motivated to be advocates, not experts. For some senators, in fact, "knowing too much" may make their lives more difficult when they are pressured into supporting something that they do not believe is the best policy, but which helps them to get reelected. They may feel that they are better off not knowing a great deal about what they are voting for on such occasions.

Obviously, there is a large problem here: How do we ensure that people in government possess the expertise required of them?

Reduce The Size Of Government

For many different reasons, the only realistic solution is to reduce the size of government to such an extent that the problem of placing experts in policymaking positions is minimized. The problem will never go away entirely. Governments do need to play a role in setting policies in numerous areas, but in today's world governments do much more than they ought to do, especially at the national level.

As regards farming—as just one example—the ideal of limited, capitalistic government defended in this book has no place for a federal farm policy that subsidizes any areas of farming, or seeks to set or to influence any farm prices, or provides any incentives to farmers by means of tax credits or low interest loans, or shelters any farm products from competition by means of tariffs or quotas. Doing any of these things introduces many more harmful incentives than beneficial incentives, especially over the long term, where the best way to strengthen American farming is not to shelter it in any way from market forces either at home or abroad. Thus, a major shrinkage of the federal government's role in relation to farming is needed. A similar shrinkage is needed in every other area where the federal government presently has policies in place that seriously undermine the incentives of a free market.

Eliminating farm subsidies would also save the federal government a lot of money, thus helping to reduce the federal debt.

If the government was prohibited from granting any special favors to farmers or farm interest groups, there would be no incentives for anyone to vote for "farm candidates" at election time. People would have incentives to vote for candidates who promise to make *the government* run better. In order to run their farms well, it would be the owner's responsibility to establish a good business system—effective marketing practices, incentives for employees to be productive and innovative, incentives for customers to pay their bills on time. Government would remain in the background where it belongs.

If my New Direction for Capitalism existed, or something close to it, the federal government would be so much smaller than it is at the present time that it would be realistic to suppose that government might come close to mastering the jobs assigned to it. The problem of how to go about placing experts in government in all of the areas where they are needed would shrink down to a manageable size. The same conclusion applies at the state level, only on a smaller scale.

West Virginia

West Virginia does not possess anything like the federal government's farm program, nor do other states, but West Virginia does maintain an extensive program for tax credits, or selective tax incentives, which is a typical example of how state governments intervene unproductively in the marketplace. The basic rationale for having such a program is to motivate new businesses to locate within one's own state, or get existing businesses to expand, by offering these businesses special deals on their taxes. There are three main reasons why these programs ought to be eliminated.

First, when such programs have been studied at the national level, few if any benefits have been found. The original expectations for creating more or better jobs by offering tax credits have almost never come close to being realized, and this is to be expected. A tax credit or other tax incentive is needed only in situations where a company would not decide on its own to move to West Virginia (or some other state); but such situations will exist only when company managers or owners judge that moving to West Virginia is not the most profitable option for the company at the time in question. Thus, a nonmarket reason to move is needed as an additional incentive, but this means that if the tax credit expires or the economic climate changes, the company is not likely to remain in West Virginia since, after all, the company managers judged originally that their business was not a particularly good fit. Yet, if the tax credit continues indefinitely, then West Virginia (or a particular region of West Virginia) must effectively continue to subsidize the company while providing the same levels of services for the company that other companies receive that pay the full amount of their taxes. The difference in revenue must come from somewhere, and most likely from the pockets of individuals or companies that could otherwise have used the money in support of businesses that did not require a subsidy to move here or expand their operations here—in other words, businesses that are a better fit for West Virginia than the ones receiving the tax credits.

Second, there is the problem of expertise in government, on which I am focusing in this chapter. Do state legislators possess the expertise needed when deciding which businesses or types of business, from all of the possible candidates, would likely work out best if given a tax break? Unhappily, there is little reason to believe that they do since the underlying economic factors involved in starting or expanding a business are complex—so much so that business people themselves who devote their lives to studying these factors often make mistakes. There is no getting around the fact that it can be very difficult to predict how well a business will do in a new location or when its operations are expanded. Yet, unless state legislators are experts in predicting which businesses or types of business are most likely to be a good fit for their state, or for a particular region of the state, they will almost certainly not make the right economic decisions when they play favorites in their attempts to create or to keep new and better jobs for West Virginia.

Third, there is the problem of fairness in the exercise of governmental power. As a matter of basic morality and regardless of their levels of expertise, government officials should not be playing favorites in the first place, but instead should be doing their best for all businesses, both the new ones and the existing ones. The very idea of a tax credit is unfair: When a new business is given a tax break, it is at the expense of existing businesses that may end up competing against the new business for customers, employees, suppliers, resources, facilities, and in other ways as well. I say more about selective tax incentives in West Virginia in Chapter 11.

Consumers As Experts

The private sector is much more likely to have experts placed where they are needed than is the public sector. One reason for this is that consumers automatically function as experts within an appropriately narrow domain.

In any society, business-related decisions must be made all the time, not just about where a company might locate a new branch, but regarding what to produce, in what quantities, when, for which markets, at what levels of quality, and so on. Answers must be found for every pencil, pair of pants, automobile, TV program, and item on a restaurant menu. In a free market, these questions are answered almost entirely on the basis of "consumer voting," which I mentioned in Chapter 3. Every time someone pays for a product or service, in effect they are casting a vote for that particular product or service. In doing this, every consumer functions as an expert within the narrow domain of that person's own preferences and values where it is realistic to suppose that a person can genuinely function as an expert, at least much of the time. People who run businesses then effectively tally all of these votes that are cast by consumers.

Of course, many consumers are experts in a broader sense than this. But the important point is that consumers do not need to be experts regarding any broad policy areas in order to cast responsible and informed consumer votes for products and services. Consumers do not need to know much about farming in general, for example, in order to cast informed votes for the farm products that they wish to buy. They need only keep themselves informed about such matters as the healthfulness of various types of food, their own special dietary needs, comparative pricing of food items at nearby stores, and some of the environmental and ethical implications of various farming practices.

Consumer votes in all areas play an immensely important economic role in setting prices not just for goods and services but also for materials, labor, facilities, and everything else that goes toward producing goods and services. The market-established prices for all of these things in relation to one another constitute an important set of incentives for economic decision-making on the part of business managers and owners, including major decisions such as where to locate a new business, along with a myriad of smaller economic decisions.

Suppose that managers of factories did not know who was actually buying what or exactly how quickly products were being sold or for how much. How would the managers begin to determine what to produce or what prices to charge? Without the detailed information provided by prices, how would managers make informed decisions? How would managers function as experts in doing their jobs? From knowledge of health and nutrition, they might infer that people ought to eat more fruit than ice cream, or ought to spend more money on vitamins and supplements than on wine. But this approach would yield precious little information for producers to go on, particularly as regards the millions of small decisions made constantly by consumers.

Should the owners of a clothing factory produce thirty percent blue flannel shirts and twenty percent red for the upcoming Christmas market, or should it be twenty percent red and thirty percent blue? Should the owners of a chain of supermarkets offer to sell apples this week at ten cents less per pound than last week because they have too many apples on hand and apples are perishable, should they cancel an order for more apples set to arrive later in the week, or will a sale on apples today increase demand enough to warrant the order for more? Without constant, direct feedback from consumers, how could factory owners, farmers, oil company executives, managers of rental agencies, university administrators, and on and on, have any significant amount of worthwhile information on which to base decisions as to what they should offer to the public or how much they should charge?

Without constant input from the market, what happens is that someone else decides *for us* the proportion of carrots to lettuce that we will eat or that will be available for us to eat. Somebody else decides whether a new type of contact lens will be offered for sale. Someone else decides what sorts of cars we will drive. Not only does the system suffer from a shortage of information, but the information that is available represents someone else's idea of what is good for us—or good for them. This is overwhelmingly true under socialist governments. It is true, though to a lesser extent, under the varieties of mixed economies that presently exist in the United States and most other countries around the world where governments play large roles in establishing farm policies, industrial policies, energy policies, and so on.

Please bear in mind that "government experts" owe their jobs primarily to political incentives, not the economic incentives of the market. Friedrich Hayek, a Nobel prizewinning economist whom I mentioned in Chapter 3, invented the term "spontaneous order" to describe a free market. Consumers' choices in the marketplace provide business managers with essential information not obtainable in any other way. Decisions of managers and investors that are a response to consumers' choices also serve an informational role that cannot be duplicated outside the marketplace. Various levels of information become intricately intertwined and extremely sensitive to changes from within any part of the overall economy. Interrelationships among consumers, producers, suppliers, workers, investors, and others in a free market are spontaneous in the sense that the resulting economic order arises from within the economy itself and is not imposed from outside by government planners. It is an ordering of production, distribution, pricing, design, investment, planning for the near and distant future, and other factors that no individual person can comprehend or needs to comprehend in its entirety. It is a system that works much more efficiently than any alternative.

The real beauty of the spontaneous order of the marketplace is that no one needs to be an expert regarding the entirety of the economic order, or anything close to it. The spontaneous order of a free market is held together by a vast, finely-tuned, interdependent, ever-changing, and very efficient network of economic incentives that come into existence "all by themselves."

Political Incentives Versus Expert Advice

If elected to their positions, government officials are strongly motivated to be reelected. But there is no reason to believe that a politician's desire to be reelected will help the general cause of economic success in a country or a state. There is, for example, no necessary connection between a politician's desire to be reelected and the goal of making West Virginia more business-friendly. If an elected official depends for support on a particular industry, then the official has a powerful incentive to support that industry at the expense of the economy as a whole. For example, the official may be under pressure to support various tariffs and quotas on imports even though they are overall bad for consumers and bad for the economy. In the long run, the tariffs will probably destroy the industry they were intended to protect, and for an obvious reason: The real motivation for the tariffs was to protect certain individuals who gave money at election time, not the industry as a whole.

As just one example, the United States has attempted for a great many years to protect the domestic textile industry with major tariffs that go back to the early nineteenth century. In 1816, the U.S. imposed a tariff of 83% on certain cotton goods, and in 1828 a tariff of 150% on woolens—the infamous "Tariff of Abominations." Tariffs on textiles were high during the 1930s, strengthened under the Kennedy and Nixon administrations, and expanded even further under the Reagan administration. The final result: The U.S. succeeded in undermining incentives from international competition that were needed to keep domestic textiles on the cutting edge. It should not be a surprise to anyone that the National Cotton Council of America described the U.S. textile industry in 2006 as an "industry in crisis."

This is not to say that the U.S. should unilaterally reduce tariffs, except in unusual circumstances. The U.S. needs to be a tough and aggressive negotiator in going after the best trade agreements that protect the interests of both American producers and American consumers. The basic strategy of the United States should be to say to one (or more) other countries: If you join with us in reducing trade and investment barriers, including government subsidies, both for products that you sell in our country and products that we sell in your country, our countries will each be better off, and together we will possess a competitive advantage over nations that are not a party to our agreement.

A Final Word

The capitalistic ideal for limited government makes a lot of sense when it is given a fair hearing. This does not usually happen. In the next chapter, I explain why spreading the word regarding capitalism has always been—and continues to be— immensely difficult.

Chapter 7.
Spreading the Word—A Huge Challenge

If capitalism is as good as my description of it in earlier chapters suggests, why aren't greater numbers of people aware that this is so?

Part of the answer is that capitalism needs to be defended in a new way, which is the main goal of this book. But there is more to the answer than that because my new way of defending capitalism is not entirely new, needless to say. Many of the points that I make—indeed, the strongest parts of my defense for capitalism—have been available for a long time. Even the old ways of defending capitalism are very much underappreciated in today's world. For example, as a university professor I encounter relatively few students who, before I discuss any of the relevant issues with them, are familiar with the milestones in the defense of capitalism that I mentioned in Chapter 3.

The most important part of the answer to the above question is that defending capitalism in today's world faces a number of serious challenges.

The Challenge From Democracy

In the United States, which is typical, the strongest incentives at election times are for voters to choose candidates who promise to benefit them, the voters, even if the policies supported by the candidates are likely to be harmful in terms of the broader picture. Politicians do little to enlighten voters because the politicians themselves face strong incentives that count against telling voters the complete truth.

As an illustration, the American system of farm price supports and controls, which I discussed in Chapter 6, unquestionably needs to be changed. America's farm policy is extremely inefficient and unfair, and is a huge roadblock to full participation by the United States in the international trade of agricultural products and technologies. The U.S. government should begin now to negotiate aggressively with other countries to achieve reductions in farm supports around the world. Phasing out farm price supports and other farming-oriented interventions by government would help consumers and taxpayers a great deal, and this fact has been known and publicized for many years. For example, according to James Bovard in *The Fair Trade Fraud*, published in 1991, the U.S. government spent more than one million dollars for every full-time American rice grower between 1985 and 1990. It spent almost a billion dollars in 1986 alone. During the 1980s, the U.S. spent a total of $260 billion in farm supports. In 1986, Turkey resold subsidized American wheat at a profit, which was paid for by American taxpayers and consumers. Bovard noted that "American wheat is cheaper in Moscow than in Minneapolis, American barley is cheaper in Baghdad than in Boston."

The point that I want to focus on here is that American farm price supports have not declined in the years following the publication of Bovard's book, which is one of several published during the past twenty years that make a compelling case against America's ongoing farm policies. Virtually nothing has been done through trade negotiations to coordinate reductions in farm support programs at home with reductions abroad, which is the most advantageous way for the U.S. to proceed. Yet, phasing out farm price supports would save a lot of money and would ultimately help American farming as a whole by making it more competitive internationally. American farmers would have stronger incentives for developing and using cutting-edge technologies and better management systems. Other nations would no longer feel the need to retaliate against the United States by maintaining their own farm supports and imposing trade restrictions on agricultural products from the U.S. Farmers in developing nations would not need to compete against subsidized farm products from the U.S., which would allow these farmers to meet the needs of their people better, and this in turn would help to promote political stability in those countries. All of this has been known for decades.

Yet, under our present system, numerous individual farmers in the United States have strong, immediate incentives to vote for maintaining and even strengthening the American farm program because their own farms have come to depend on it. These farmers therefore have strong incentives to give money to politicians who support the present system. Many farmers have invested in land and equipment against the prospect of selling their harvests at artificial prices; we can certainly understand why they have done this given the present situation. Politicians in farm states have strong incentives to play into the fears of their constituents, which they do by defending both the U.S. farm program and the concept of big government. It would be inconsistent to defend the first but not the second. These same politicians do *not* have incentives to learn more about the harm done by the U.S. farm program or to learn more about other problems belonging to the type of economic system that permits farm price supports. Because incentives make the world go round, it is fair to say that these politicians are held captive by the incentives currently in place within our democratic political system, and the same is true regarding a great many voters.

Do people who are not farmers or politicians living in farm states have incentives to vote for phasing out the U.S. farm program? Of course they do. But first these people must come to understand how the U.S. farm program actually works. Few politicians wish to educate voters because the present system keeps the politicians in power. Journalists who cover politics mostly report what various politicians and their supporters are saying, so journalists do not help much, with some exceptions. Consequently, the truth about free market economics in relation to farming, as well as other domains of life, remains largely hidden from large numbers of voters.

Furthermore, even if a majority of voters did learn how farm supports actually work, their strongest and most immediate incentives would still be to vote for candidates who serve the voters' interests more directly and immediately: as bankers, borrowers, butchers, steel makers, steel users, steel workers, union members, teachers, professors, doctors, lawyers, insurance executives, employees of airlines, employees of the U.S. Postal Service, the rich, the poor, the unemployed, etc. Because the U.S. government exercises such extensive powers, politicians are in a position to do special favors for all of these groups and numerous others. Politicians are also in a position to support programs and policies that can *harm* the interests of all of these groups. In fact, everyone belongs to multiple groups that politicians at election times can promise to help or potentially can hurt. Thus, incentives for genuine reform of the governmental system as a whole, or even for important parts of the system, are almost always overshadowed in the minds of voters by more powerful or more immediate disincentives. Incentives for people *to learn about* the requirements for genuine reform are also usually overshadowed by disincentives.

This is a problem of huge magnitude. "The truth shall set you free." Yes, indeed. Truth about economic and political realities can save Americans from the otherwise likely prospect of a declining standard of living in the years to come. Economic and political truth can make West Virginia the most prosperous state in the country and the best place to live. But first, the truth must become widely known across the country and within West Virginia. That will not happen unless the American people in general and West Virginians in particular break free from a powerful set of incentives and disincentives that count against spreading the word about the best versions of capitalistic government.

Can this be done?

Yes, it can be done. There is only one requirement—that voters come to understand how capitalism actually works when capitalism is given the strongest possible defense. This is where my New Direction for Capitalism enters the picture. This is where the book you are now reading becomes relevant because capitalism can be defended in a new and stronger way—the main goal of this book.

Within the United States at the present time, a failure to fully understand capitalistic government at its best is a powerful brake on achieving the level of economic success that is required if we are to overcome the financial handicaps inherited from our recent and not-so-recent past, especially a gigantic federal debt and huge federal entitlement programs upon which so many people depend. Without a robust economy, which requires that voters understand capitalism at its best in order to support measures that will strengthen the economy now *and long-term*, the federal debt will inevitably give rise to greatly increased taxes and/or high rates of inflation, both of which will further hurt the U.S. economy. It will then be even more difficult for the U.S. to pay the interest on its debt, which in turn will require more borrowing by the government—and at higher rates of interest as the U.S. becomes less creditworthy. A downward spiral will overtake us. Higher tax rates and/or increasing inflation, if not stopped in time, will be disastrous for the United States.

We as a society face a make-it-or-break-it choice: We can wait until it is too late for an understanding of capitalistic ideas to give us a strong competitive edge early on when it will count the most against other countries, or we can begin now to include the right kinds of support for capitalism in politicians' speeches, media coverage of current events, and the word of mouth propagation of ideas. We can begin now to move toward a time when a majority of American voters feel completely comfortable with all of the essential ideas pertaining to capitalism at its best. We can begin now to move as quickly as possibly toward a time when West Virginia's voters feel completely comfortable with these ideas.

As citizens of West Virginia, let us set an example for the rest of the country.

The Challenge From A Lack Of Awareness Of "What Might Have Been"

Typically, as unintended bad consequences, interventions in people's lives by big government either prevent or discourage good things from happening. These unintended bad consequences must be taken into account if there is to be an accurate determination of whether or not the interventions are a good thing overall. But it is extremely difficult to measure "what might have been." Most government interventions do produce some benefits for some people, at least temporarily, and these benefits exist for everyone to see—this subsidy, that loan guarantee, this tax credit, that protective tariff, this regulation that favors a particular business or industry, that infusion of bailout money into the economy of a particular region.

What about the new business that would have come into existence if additional taxes had not drained away the resources required to finance it? What about the jobs that would have come into existence if increased taxes and compliance costs for numerous regulations had not prevented a company from expanding? What about the new medical discovery that would have been made if greater freedom to pursue it had existed? What about the individuals who would have become physicians and served in rural areas if some of the barriers to entry into medicine had not existed? All of these businesses, benefits, and careers are ghosts. They are invisible to the eyes of nearly everyone. They are never mentioned by the politicians who brag about all the marvelous things they have done while spending other people's money.

The sad fact is that relatively few people have incentives to seek knowledge about what might have been, while powerful incentives exist for spreading the word about the supposed positive accomplishments of typical politicians.

One of the best illustrations of what might have been is employment. Everyone agrees that high levels of unemployment are bad, both for society as a whole and for the people who do not have jobs. (Low levels of unemployment, at perhaps three percent of the work force, are necessary for the smooth operation of an efficient economy, because they allow for normal job turnover and the flexibility required for new businesses to start up.) Well-meaning individuals say: Government ought to do something about high levels of unemployment. It should hire people for public service projects or train people for jobs in the public and private sectors. It should dispense large amounts of "stimulus money" for the purpose of creating jobs. Government should make up for the supposed inadequacies of a free market. Seldom considered is the fact that high levels of unemployment are usually caused by government interventions in the first place: Trade barriers, high taxes, zillions of regulations, huge compliance costs pertaining to vast numbers of laws and complex tax codes, mistakes by the Federal Reserve that precipitate or lengthen recessions. All of these greatly increase unemployment.

What are the likely consequences of government actions intended specifically to reduce unemployment?

Suppose government hires people directly or supplies funds for companies in the private sector to hire people. That will cost money. Suppose the government trains people for jobs either in the public or private sectors. That too will cost money. But there exists only one ultimate source for this money: the private sector. If the money is taken through taxes, then businesses will have less available to use for payrolls and expansion, or else consumers will have less to spend, depending on who pays the taxes. If it is consumers who pay, there will be a decrease in the need for more workers to be hired in order to produce the goods or services that the consumers would have bought if their money had not been taken in taxes. If the money is obtained by government through less direct channels such as borrowing or increasing the money supply via the Federal Reserve, thereby raising the level of inflation, then the over-all result will still be the same—a net loss of available investment capital or buying power in the private sector. That means fewer jobs in the private sector.

Advocates of government employment programs never mention the jobs that might have been. Politicians who give speeches about all the jobs they are creating via government programs are either ignorant (because they do not possess the incentives needed to gain the requisite knowledge) or believe that they have good reasons for hiding the truth. But if they hide the truth, and journalists follow in their wake, then the citizens of a country will likely not come to learn the truth.

In addition, many people—especially those who actually obtain government-created jobs (jobs that are typically created at the expense of other jobs that would have come into existence absent the efforts of government)—possess strong incentives that count against supporting efforts that would make other people aware of all of the jobs that might have been. I do not mean to suggest that public employees do not play very important roles in numerous areas. We do need public employees in many walks of life. My point is that public employee's jobs largely ride piggyback on private sector jobs that provide money through taxes and fees to pay the salaries of public employees. The bedrock of employment is always the private sector.

The moral of this story is simple: Everyone who lives in a democracy has a civic duty to master thoroughly the concept of "what might have been" as it applies to government spending, especially in the area of employment, and to help others gain a mastery of this concept. Let us in West Virginia take the lead in becoming informed about this important concept.

I turn next to another dimension of the challenge faced by anyone who wishes to spread the word in defense of strengthening capitalism.

The Challenge From Bad Behavior

I will begin with a question: Is there too much freedom in today's world?

Let me say first that my own firmly held belief is that the answer to this question is an emphatic no. But I do understand why people might believe otherwise when they look around and observe that large numbers of people are behaving badly in today's world, either as criminals or as individuals who stay inside the law but behave unethically. Capitalism is rightly associated with the concept of freedom: Generally speaking, the more capitalism that we have, the more that people are left alone to conduct their businesses and their lives as they see fit. Capitalism does require the enforcement of laws to protect basic rights—laws against theft, fraud, the violation of contracts, slander, violent acts of all kinds, threats of violence, actions that harm the environment or threaten public health or safety, and others. These are laws that limit freedom for the sake of protecting freedom. NDC also requires laws and programs pertaining to helping people in need and making society as a whole a better place. But for all capitalistic societies, government plays a substantially smaller role in telling us what we can and cannot do than is true for non-capitalistic societies.

Therefore, if a great many people are behaving badly, it may begin to make sense to wonder whether there might be too much freedom, and hence too much capitalism. We may begin to wonder whether the bad behavior that we see in the news everyday could be lessened if people were kept on a tighter leash. If we have this thought in the back of our mind, we may be less open to being persuaded that capitalism should be reinvigorated along the lines of NDC. We may feel impelled to speak out against strengthening capitalism, and attempt to persuade others to do likewise. This is especially likely to happen when there are numerous current news stories about misconduct on Wall Street and by corporate owners and managers.

Indeed, there are news stories every day about misconduct not only in business and government, but also in the world of sports and by celebrities in many fields. TV shows and personal advice columns feature misconduct in families, between friends, and within communities. There are news stories about serious misconduct in the schools, even elementary schools. There are stories about Internet scams, con artists using the Postal Service, and fraudulent home repair people going from door to door. At the present time there are new categories of crime, such as identity theft and the creation of computer viruses. And of course the worst kinds of misconduct are violent crimes of all types.

Seeing all this, many people come to possess a mind set that works against spreading the word about the true strengths of capitalism. Instead, people want to clamp down on conduct of many different types, and they perceive that increasing the powers of government to "legislate morality" is the best way to accomplish this.

The position taken in this book is that a much better alternative is to combine support for capitalism, where the protection of freedom is strengthened, and support for moral values. In Chapter 8, I say more about the details of this combination. My point here is that restricting people's freedom beyond what is required by my New Direction for Capitalism is not the best way to get people to behave better. History teaches us that less free countries are usually not more moral countries. As an extreme example, communist countries were notoriously corrupt and racist. By contrast, capitalistic societies contain strong incentives for people to put aside their prejudices in order to hire the best people to do the job at hand, regardless of the race, gender, religion, etc., of the individuals who are hired. The more that competition is open, the less that a company can afford to hire on the basis of prejudice in an uneconomical fashion. Likewise, capitalistic societies contain strong incentives for people in business to put aside their prejudices in order to reach the widest possible market for selling goods and services. Talent, a willingness to work hard, and a willingness to spend money are great levelers within a free market society, and so also are the opportunities that everyone has in a free society to speak out, organize, raise money, and otherwise devote themselves to fighting against the existence of bigotry and prejudice.

At the same time, it must be noted that in years gone by, as I said in Chapter 2, the incentives within capitalistic societies for people to put aside their prejudices were not always strong enough to overcome the even greater strengths of those prejudices themselves—which is why affirmative action laws were needed and beneficial during the second half of the twentieth century. To arrive at the point where American society now finds itself in the 21st century—where the benefits of capitalism are much more readily and fairly available to members of all groups—required an activist government during the second half of the twentieth that was not in the spirit of NDC, except in the sense that NDC-guided government is given a mandate to exercise a greater level of governmental power and control during times of emergency than it normally exercises. A case can be made for describing the treatment of African Americans, women, and members of other disadvantaged groups prior to the successes of all of the different 20th century rights movements as constituting an emergency, in the same way that the American Civil War can be described as a response to the emergency of American slavery that was deeply entrenched in several southern states prior to the war. The point to be emphasized here is that the benefits of capitalism at the present time *are* much more readily and fairly available to members of all groups. The emergency is past. We no longer need to invoke such extensive powers of government in order to get people to behave morally in the relevant areas. We can instead rely on voluntary morality, which is usually the best thing to do.

Why is voluntary morality usually best? One reason is that making moral decisions often requires finding the right balance among competing moral demands. It may require weighing one's own happiness against the special needs of individuals and against the good of society, and sometimes weighing each of the latter against the others. I say more about this balancing act in Chapter 8. Unquestionably, making moral decisions can be a difficult and delicate task. Governments are not well suited to handling moral complexity. The system of incentives built into government is inherently too heavy-handed, on the whole, to deal effectively with moral complexity. What government does especially well is provide a secure setting within which *individuals* can make difficult moral decisions.

The conclusion I wish to draw, then, is that the "challenge from bad behavior" is not a good reason at the present time to oppose the strengthening of capitalism.

The Challenge From Widely Held Beliefs

I turn now to another facet of the problem of spreading the word about capitalism.

Many people do not think about the strengths of free enterprise when they think about capitalism, but instead think about "greedy capitalists." Spreading the word about the importance of strengthening capitalism requires that this association of ideas be overcome.

Let us ask: What sort of person is a capitalist? The answer that large numbers of people might give is that capitalists want to make money more than anything else. They are "rugged individualists" who believe in a world of rough-and-tumble competition where people must fend for themselves. At election times, they vote for candidates who are "friends of big business" and can be expected to grant special favors to businesses that donate generously at election times. They are strong-willed individuals—tough, even ruthless. Ideas such as these have become associated with the word "capitalist" in the minds of many people.

As I mentioned in earlier chapters, some of the blame for this state of affairs lies with Adam Smith, Ayn Rand, Milton Friedman, and other influential writers who convey the impression that capitalism is inconsistent with widely held moral values, especially concern for people in need and for the well-being of society as a whole. Capitalism has frequently been portrayed as cold and harsh. Rand defends capitalism in conjunction with the view that everyone ought to seek their own happiness ahead of everything else. This is a view that philosophers call ethical, or normative, egoism. Smith, the eighteenth century author of *The Wealth of Nations* to whom all contemporary advocates of capitalism are indebted, did not advocate normative egoism, which says that people *ought* to put self-interest first, but appealed instead to the idea that people *do as a matter of human nature* put self-interest first. The name given by philosophers to this second version of egoism is "psychological egoism." Capitalism is the best economic and political system, according to this point of view, because it puts all of the inevitable self-interest to work for the good of society as a whole.

Although Smith himself did not explicitly say such a thing, his defense capitalism is often viewed as giving a free pass for just about any efforts, as long as they are legal, that people might make within a free market to produce a profit. There is some justification for this reading of Smith since he does say the following in *The Wealth of Nations*: "I have never known much good done by those who affected to trade for the public good." This reading of Smith's doctrine of the Invisible Hand is echoed by Ludwig von Mises, one of the twentieth century's most influential defenders of free markets. Mises says the following in his *Liberalism in the Classical Tradition*, published in 1927:

> The manager of a private enterprise gives the employees to whom he assigns independent duties only one directive: to make as much profit as possible. Everything that he has to say to them is comprehended in this one order.

Mises' point is echoed by Milton Friedman, whose views I have discussed in earlier chapters.

Many things can be said in response to the unfortunate assertions about capitalism made by Rand, Smith, Mises, Friedman, and others. First and foremost, we must keep in mind the fact that Smith's doctrine of the Invisible Hand expresses only a partial truth. Unquestionably, capitalism does *tend* to convert the pursuit of self-interest by numerous individuals into the betterment of society, and it does so much more effectively than any alternatives. Government bureaucracies are the worst among alternatives. But Smith's doctrine of the Invisible Hand is too strong because there are many ways for people in business to make profits without providing consumers with goods or services that are genuinely beneficial. The Invisible

101

Hand does not guide the makers and sellers of the worst sorts of junk food, useless cold medications, tobacco products, etc., to make society a better place! Thus, while there is a lot of truth to Smith's doctrine of the Invisible Hand, it does not contain the full picture.

The most important response that we can make to statements about capitalism from Rand, Smith, Mises, and others is to locate capitalistic ideas and ideals within the context of the best moral ideas and ideals, which is what I do in the next chapter. Doing this will support spreading the word about capitalism at its best to as many people as possible.

Chapter 8.
Morality First, Government Second

I begin with a question. Why should we care whether or not the best economic and political system exists? The answer, I am sure, will be obvious to readers of this book: We want people's lives to go as well as possible. That is the fundamental reason why we want every state and every country, not just our own, to have the best system of government. (Of course, it would be nice if our own state and our own country got there first!)

Why do we want the lives of everyone to go well? The answer is that we are committed to basic moral values of concern for our fellow human beings.

Nothing is more important in today's turbulent world than morality. One reason is that a moral life is the most satisfying life: Not the easiest life, but the best, and the best in ways that count for the most over the long term. Most of us know this, at least in the back of our minds, or we are reminded of it from time to time by events in our own lives or the lives of others. Likewise, we are often reminded that the temptation "just this once" to do something morally wrong has destroyed countless careers.

Even greater harm lies elsewhere, especially in situations where an immoral outlook on life leads to criminal conduct.

For example, according to a 2007 survey by the National Retail Federation, shoplifting costs American consumers $25 billion a year. According to a report in 2006 by the National Prison Commission, the American prison system costs $60 billion a year. Shoplifting and the prison system are examples where actual dollar figures can be assigned for money that either is lost outright or is spent in an effort to prevent even greater harm.

In other types of situations, no dollar figure can be assigned because the money lost belongs to "what might have been" if people had not behaved badly. "What might have been" in this context is hard to determine because the sorts of honorable, successful activities that are blocked by bad behavior usually have multiplier effects upon other honorable, successful activities, and these are difficult to track. For example, corporate management practices that treat employees with disrespect often lose money for companies because employees do not perform at their best when they are treated disrespectfully. By contrast, if the companies had treated their employees better, and had been more successful as a consequence, that success would doubtless have rubbed off on other companies or individuals doing business with the original company. The success would have rubbed off on the employees of the original company as well, who probably would have ended up being paid more, and also feeling much more satisfied with their jobs and their lives. Instead, all of these benefits were lost because of the ripple effects of the original bad behavior.

In still other situations, what is lost as the result of immoral behavior is not the sort of thing to which a dollar value can even begin to be assigned, such as when family relationships or friendships are destroyed. Likewise, when the level of corruption among people in government or business increases, there is often no way to assign a monetary value to the harm that results. The same is true regarding the increased levels of insecurity and fear that result from higher rates of burglary, fraud, identity theft, assault, drug-related violence, and the acts of terrorists against innocent people.

Improving moral understanding and behavior will give us (to mention just some of the benefits): better businesses, friendships, marriages, communities, schools, and institutions of all types; the saving of vast amounts of money in the many areas of life where money is now lost to fraud, theft, or corruption; more safety and security at all levels of society; less violence around the world; the satisfaction of knowing at the end of one's life that it has been lived well—because it has been lived morally—regardless of how one's life may be measured against other standards of success.

Better Moral Understanding, Better Government

Most important of all, improving moral behavior and understanding will give us better governments with large benefits accruing to everyone. However, there is a long-standing problem, namely that people's views about morality have usually been inadequate where government is concerned.

The most extreme example is socialism, where the basic moral goal is to ensure that the needs of everyone are met. For Karl Marx, the slogan "from each according to ability, to each according to need" was intended to express a profound moral truth. But when put into practice via socialist governments, this slogan turned out to be a disaster. In socialist societies, people's needs are not met adequately (far from it), people's basic rights are routinely violated, and governments are always corrupt. Even milder attempts by government to meet people's needs often work out badly, as with the federal government's interventions in mortgage banking that played a large role in the economic downturn that began in 2008 and continues to be felt at the present time. These interventions were originally intended to increase home ownership among people with low incomes, which in itself is a worthy moral goal. Likewise, public housing projects in numerous large American cities were motivated by worthy moral goals but were almost all failures. One of the important lessons to be learned here is that moral goals that are worthy in *themselves* may nevertheless yield a lot more harm than good when they are pursued outside of a more comprehensive moral viewpoint such as I describe later in this chapter.

Another example where the views of many people regarding morality in connection with government are inadequate involves the circumstances for the 2005 Supreme Court decision *Kelo v. New London*. In this 5-4 decision, the Court upheld the city of New London, Connecticut, in its use of the power of eminent domain to take Susan Kelo's personal residence in order to give the land on which the house stood, along with other land in the neighborhood, to a private developer. The resulting development, it was said, would bring in a lot more tax revenue and create jobs for the area. It would serve the greater good, which in itself is a worthy moral goal. However, *Kelo v. New London* received much criticism across the country on Constitutional grounds, as it should have. There is little reason to believe that the framers of the Constitution intended to include such situations as *Kelo* when they wrote the Fifth Amendment's Takings Clause, which allows private property to be taken for "public use," as when a road is built. On purely moral grounds as well, the position of the Court in *Kelo* is problematic, and for the following reason.

Acting for the sake of the good of society (the "greater good," or even the "greatest good for the greatest number") without sufficient regard for other moral values such as the protection of property rights and/or helping people in need is dangerous because it is likely to promote an indifference to the well-being of individuals like Susan Kelo. As a matter of history, people in positions of power and influence have all too often invoked the idea of the greater good as a pretext for suppressing their enemies or ridding the world of "unworthy minorities." It is dangerous to defend any government institutions or policies by an unqualified appeal to the good of society because doing so will seem to give legitimacy to government actions that someone somewhere *claims* will bring about the greatest good for society. What is needed as a safeguard is an *independent moral commitment* to the protection of basic rights, along with other foundational moral values.

As I have said in earlier chapters, this book is committed to the view that government should play a limited role in ensuring that the good of society is served even when this means that some basic rights, such as property rights, are not fully upheld. Likewise, government should play a limited role in helping people in need even if, again, this means that some basic rights are not fully upheld. However, the only way for such governmental roles to remain properly limited is for enough people—voters and opinion-makers especially—to come to agree that government should place *much more weight* on the protection of basic rights than on other moral values. In short, enough people must come to agree that the NDC model for strictly limited government, or something close to it, ought to be followed. Otherwise, encroachments upon rights will become even greater. Taxes and red tape will become an even larger burden.

Because the point that I just made is so important, I will repeat it: When it comes to helping people in need and enhancing the good of society as a whole, which are important moral goals in themselves, the only way for government's role to remain sufficiently modest in scope is for enough people to understand that government should place much more weight on the protection of basic rights than on these other two worthy moral values. Informed voters are the key. And the key to having informed voters is the availability of a comprehensive view of morality that can stand on its own as a guide to life and that can also serve as a foundation for the best type of government.

Where should we start?

The Intrinsic Value Of All Human Lives

I can think of no better starting place than the observation that human lives have intrinsic value, by which is meant that human lives have value in themselves. From a religious perspective, the intrinsic value of human lives can be expressed by saying that all human beings are "precious in the eyes of God."

Suppose someone says: "I do not believe that everyone's life has intrinsic value. *My life* has intrinsic value. It has value to me. As regards other people's lives, I do not see why I should care about them unless they serve my interests. If capitalistic government is best for me, that is why I want it, period. I do not see why I also have an obligation to help people in need or contribute to the well-being of society as a whole." The person who says these things is an egoist.

Josiah Royce, an American philosopher of the late nineteenth and early twentieth centuries, gave what I believe is the best reply to the egoist. Other people are "selves like me," said Royce. They feel pain and joy and sorrow the same as I do. The people whom I pass in the street possess hopes and fears and desires, dreams and secret ambitions and disappointments, just as I do. They are conscious centers of experience in the same way that I am, meaning that each possesses an inner life of thought and feeling that exists for them just as my inner life of thought and feeling exists for me. The following is from Royce's *The Religious Aspects of Philosophy*, published in 1885:

> If he is like thee, then is his life as bright a light, as warm a fire, to him, as thine to thee; his will is as full of struggling desires, of hard problems, of fateful decisions; his pains are as hateful, his joys as dear.

Royce is saying, essentially, that if my life has intrinsic value, then so do the lives of everyone else. The recognition that all human beings are "selves like me" can be called *Royce's Insight*. Yet, throughout much of the world's history, Royce's Insight has been neglected—trampled into the mud, if the truth be told.

A Brief Moral History

Until relatively recent times, most of the world's cultures were essentially "tribal" in nature: Only members of one's own culture or society, as determined primarily by political, religious, or ethnic criteria, were judged to be other selves in the sense meant by Royce. People outside one's own group were judged to be foreigners, barbarians, or infidels, not full-fledged moral beings like us. It was morally acceptable to steal from them, enslave them, or kill them. Throughout history, there have been countless "tribes"—nations, provinces, city-states, races, clans, shared language-speaking groups, political groups, religious groups, socioeconomic classes, and others. While the sizes and membership of these groups have varied greatly, the underlying principle has always been the same: Human beings are not equal, and in fact—for the more extreme versions of tribalism—some human beings do not count morally at all.

The ancient Athenians at the time of Plato and Aristotle, during the "Golden Age of Athens," treated everyone who was not a Greek as fair game to be enslaved. Among the non-Greeks were the Persians, who for their part enslaved the Greeks whenever they could manage to do so. The ancient Romans drew a sharp distinction between citizens of Rome, whose rights were protected, and everyone else, whose rights were not protected. Early in their history, the Romans totally exterminated the Carthaginians, who for their part had been doing their best to conquer and enslave the Romans.

Later on, Christians killed Muslims, the Moors killed the Spanish, native North and South American tribes captured and killed warriors from other tribes, Americans and Europeans bought and sold Africans, the Bolsheviks exterminated the Kulaks, the Nazis practiced genocide, the Japanese army brutalized many Chinese people during World War II, and numerous twentieth century despots engaged in attempts at so-called ethnic cleansing. The manifestations of a "privileged group" view of morality constitute history's oldest, saddest, and most ubiquitous story.

Even within the confines of unified societies, for most of recorded history drastically different levels of recognition were granted to the selfhood of various categories of human beings, with people in one group judged to be of much greater value than people in another group. Women were almost never given the same recognition as men, nor were children granted the same recognition as adults. Parents in ancient Rome were allowed to sell their children and sometimes even to kill them. Women in Medieval Europe were the property of their husbands, and in early America were not permitted to inherit

110

property. Women in the United States were barred from entering most professions throughout all of the nineteenth century and were not allowed to vote until 1920. Members of the aristocracy in England for centuries assigned to themselves the best of everything—education, jobs, social position, wealth, and access to political power. The caste system in India exerted a profoundly negative influence for many centuries.

In virtually all societies throughout history, individuals with special problems, such as those judged to be insane, were assigned an inferior moral status or no moral status, and this was true even in quite recent times in developed nations. In most societies, individuals with unconventional ideas or beliefs were not granted full moral standing; one of "them" was not equal to one of "us." During most of recorded history, religious dissenters were persecuted for their beliefs, and frequently were killed in barbaric ways. Relatively small differences in religious beliefs were often sufficient for the existence of deeply divisive group distinctions.

Yet, over the centuries with many stops and starts along the way, there has occurred an expanding recognition of the validity of Royce's Insight—slowly at first, but gathering momentum eventually, and finally snowballing during the second half of the twentieth century. Insofar as the world has experienced genuine moral progress at a fundamental level, here is where it is to be found. Enlightened people everywhere now believe that absolutely everyone deserves recognition of their inherent worth and dignity, their equality as selves.

But only recently has this point of view come to be widely embraced. Within the span of about two generations, there has occurred the Civil Rights movement, the Women's Rights movement, and similar movements addressed to gays and lesbians, the elderly, the physically handicapped, people with mental and emotional problems, criminals, and many others. The earth now contains nearly seven billion people. Is there any reason to believe that Royce's Insight does not apply equally to all of them? Is there any reason why we should not put all of the other more limited moralities behind us once and for all?

The fact that the world has taken several thousand years to move away from limited, group-oriented moralities does not mean that Royce's Insight is difficult to grasp in itself. Almost everyone at some stage in his or her life sees the point of it as applied to at least one other person, most often a child, spouse, parent, or friend. Of course, the psychological and cognitive mechanisms involved in the recognition of another self are doubtless complex. When I am in the right frame of mind, I am sometimes struck by the wonder of the transition in understanding and feeling from myself to others! What, after all, does make it possible for me to perceive that another human being feels pain and pleasure just as I do?

I do not know the full answer to that question. Yet, I have no doubt that readers of this book understand what it means to say that another human being is a self like me.

As I said above, I know of no better foundation for morality than Royce's Insight. If we accept Royce's Insight, then we have the best of reasons for believing that everyone's life has intrinsic value. We have the best of reasons for replacing all of the limited, group-oriented moralities with *universal morality*. Universal morality applies to every human being equally just because it recognizes that everyone's life has intrinsic value.

I turn next to the all-important question of how to apply universal morality in the real world. The greatest challenge comes from the fact that worthy moral goals often conflict with one another.

Conflicting Moral Principles

It is not difficult to see that doing things that respect or support the intrinsic value of one person's life may have the opposite consequence for someone else's life. A general in battle, for example, must sometimes send soldiers to be injured or killed in order to save the lives of a greater number. The interests of an elderly taxpayer on a limited income may conflict with the interests of other taxpayers whose children go to a public school in need of expensive improvements that require a tax increase. The interests of someone whose property is condemned by an eminent domain proceeding may conflict with the interests of someone else whose company gets to build a road on the property. The interests of someone who is old, ill, and indigent, and who relies heavily on Medicaid and other types of public support may conflict with the interests of a middle-aged laborer in good health who struggles to pay his taxes, portions of which go to programs like Medicaid.

In order to be moral individuals in the fullest sense, we must be able to make correct decisions in situations where there are difficult conflicts. Tough choices often need to be made as well by legislators, state governors, presidents, and other government leaders, and also by all of the citizens who must decide which candidates to vote for at election times.

On what basis should citizens and government officials make the tough choices? The general answer is: On the basis of moral principles. But finding the right moral principles to guide us in making tough choices can be difficult. Consider the following.

British philosophers in early nineteenth century Great Britain observed that a small minority of the population, namely the members of the aristocracy, received the lion's share of benefits from society—the best schooling (frequently it was the only schooling available), the best houses, the best jobs, the best food, etc.—and occupied virtually all positions of power and influence in government and the professions. Several philosophers, Jeremy Bentham and J. S. Mill being the most prominent among them, worked out the defense for what was then the new moral philosophy of utilitarianism: Let us do everything in life for the sake of the greatest good for the greatest number (rather than for the greatest good of the smallest number—the aristocracy!). Through their efforts as philosophers and as political activists, Bentham and Mill were able to influence the policies of the British government, with beneficial results for large numbers of British citizens. Their utilitarian principle of the greatest good was a large improvement over what had been in place in earlier times. It continues to the present day to be a very influential moral principle. But for all of that, it is highly problematic. In what follows, I will first address some of the positive aspects of the principle of the greatest good. I will then address some of the negative aspects.

For people in positions of power and influence, whether in the private or public sectors, it does seem reasonable to ask of them that they pay a lot of attention to the consequences of their actions upon large numbers of people. It may not be too much to ask that they concern themselves with the greatest good for the greatest number. Certainly, corporations should seek to produce goods or services that are genuinely beneficial to consumers, and the larger the numbers of consumers who benefit, the better. Likewise, government programs, such as welfare programs intended to support people in need, should be designed to benefit large numbers of people. But to ask the same thing of us "ordinary folks" who have more mundane jobs and perhaps families to look after is clearly going too far.

114

It is asking too much of us to require that all of our actions, and all of our goals in life, be for the sake of the greatest good for the greatest number. Of course, we should do things to help others, but the Principle of the Greatest Good (as we may call it) needs to be balanced against other moral values, such as a separate duty that each of us has to look after ourselves and the people close to us. Indeed, on some occasions, all that morality seems to require of us (if we do not occupy positions of great power and influence, as most of us do not) is that we not harm other people, or in other words that we respect their basic rights.

In my opinion, nearly all of the important moral reformers throughout history have been like Bentham and Mill: They have had a single good idea, or perhaps two good ideas at most, and they have then worked tirelessly in their efforts to remake the world to reflect their good ideas. Unhappily, these good ideas have at best contained only a part of the moral truth. The resulting moral reforms have been one-sided, and, where government is concerned, this one-sidedness has seriously distorted the aims of politicians while simultaneously contributing to a widespread misunderstanding of government's proper role.

Moral Pluralism

As regards the moral dimensions of capitalism, my goal in this book is not to attempt to reduce morality to a single principle, such as the principle of the greatest good advocated by Bentham and Mill, or the principle of egoism that is Ayn Rand's starting point. I believe also that we should reject as our starting point the socialist ideal that is encapsulated in the slogan "from each according to ability, to each according to need." We should reject Milton Friedman's claim that the only responsibility of business managers is to make as much money as possible for stockholders, and we should reject the moral views

115

of libertarians who base their political thinking exclusively on the protection of basic rights.

In place of defending any attempts to reduce morality to a single basic principle, my goal in this book is to defend a philosophy of "moral pluralism" which focuses on these four basic principles:

> * Moral individuals should do what they can to improve society as a whole, or at least to improve a significant portion of society;
> * Moral individuals should do what they can to fulfill themselves and look after themselves;
> * Moral individuals should do what they can to help people in need;
> * Moral individuals should do what they can to protect the basic rights of every person.

Each of these principles contains the words "do what they can." The reason is that all four of these principles are important, but not all can be implemented, or implemented fully, in all situations. Moral individuals should do what they can toward implementing each of these principles, looked at one by one, while not ignoring the other principles. Tough moral choices sometimes need to be made, both by individual citizens and by government officials, simply because these four principles can conflict with one another. Such conflict is a defining characteristic of moral pluralism.

As understood here, moral pluralism means a view of morality where there are several different basic principles, and where there is no single underlying, or unifying, principle that resolves conflicts that may arise. The first principle on my list does resemble the principle of the greatest good that is advocated by utilitarians. The difference is that here I am treating my version of the principle of the greatest good as being *just one* among four different basic moral principles, while utilitarians treat it as being *the single* basic unifying moral principle. My version of this principle is weaker than the utilitarian version.

The second of the four principles on my list resembles the principle that Rand derives from her exclusive focus on the pursuit of each individual's own self-interest. By contrast, my focus is not exclusive: Sometimes we do need to devote most of our energies to making things better just for ourselves—especially if we have been neglecting ourselves—but just as often, when "duty calls" we should instead devote much of our time and energy to making things better for other people (and we should do this for the sake of these other people, not just to make ourselves happier).

The third of the four principles on my list resembles that portion of the socialist principle that can be expressed by the words "to each according to need." Unquestionably, this principle expresses a worthy moral goal in itself, as I said earlier; it is not an accident that so many people have found inspiration in socialism. But again, my focus here is not exclusive. It is a recognition that *sometimes* our most important moral duty is to reach out to people who are in especially great need. Other times, we should focus our energies elsewhere.

The fourth of the four principles on my list resembles the principle of rights that libertarians appeal to in their defense of libertarian government. There is a lot to be said in defense of this appeal by libertarians. I do believe that, by far, the most important function of government is the protection of basic rights to life, liberty, the ownership of property, and the pursuit of happiness. But I do not believe that protecting basic rights is the only proper function of government, which should also include efforts to help people in need and make society as a

117

whole a better place. The same moral requirement applies to the individual citizens in a country: We should do our part in respecting the basic rights of others, but this is not the only moral obligation that we have.

Once Again—The Intrinsic Value Of Human Lives

As I said earlier, nearly all of the important moral reformers throughout history have arrived at a single good idea, or perhaps two good ideas at most, and they have then devoted themselves to promoting their one or two good ideas, not recognizing that these ideas contain only a part of the moral truth. What is needed is a comprehensive moral ideal that includes all of the important moral principles that reflect the intrinsic value of human lives. This means moral pluralism of the type that I am defending here. Moral pluralism as defended here fulfills the requirements for being a version of universal morality, which is morality that applies to every human being equally because it recognizes that everyone's life has intrinsic value. It acknowledges the religious idea that is expressed in saying that everyone is precious in God's eyes. What we arrive at, therefore, is Universal Moral Pluralism.

I ask readers to reflect on each of the four basic principles listed above. You will see that each of them in its own way is oriented to the intrinsic value of human lives. Taken all together, they constitute the very best comprehensive moral ideal. They are the best moral guide for everyone's life, and they provide the best moral foundation for government. Consider the following.

The greater good. Why, if we find ourselves in a position to do so, should we work toward improving society as a whole? The answer: Because society is composed of individual human beings whose lives have intrinsic value. Doing things that support such value by making people's lives better is unquestionably morally good.

Looking after our own interests. Why should we expend a significant portion of our time and energy creating for ourselves a fulfilling life? The answer: Because our own lives have intrinsic value that will be undermined if we let ourselves down. Some philosophers express this important idea by saying that we have "self-regarding duties."

Helping people in need. Why should we make special efforts to help people in need? Again, the answer is that the lives of these individuals have intrinsic value that will be compromised if their important needs remain unmet. If we are in a position to help out, without greatly undermining our other moral obligations, we should do so.

Protecting basic rights. Why should we do what we can to help toward the protection of the basic rights of every individual, and avoid violating anyone's rights? The answer is that the lives of every human being, with no exceptions, have intrinsic value that is jeopardized when basic rights are not protected.

Overall, what Universal Moral Pluralism asks of us is that we find a balance among the values that I have just outlined. I believe that when the balance is achieved in regard to government, we will find that we have committed ourselves to my New Direction for Capitalism, or something close to it.

119

Chapter 9.
Quality and Ethics Management

Many people believe that capitalism is an amoral, dog-eat-dog system that rewards people for being greedy. This belief stems in part from the way that capitalism has been defended over the years via an association with the concept of egoism and the "pure pursuit of profit" view of business. My New Direction for Capitalism is free from this association since NDC is based on a moral philosophy—as explained in the previous Chapter—that rejects egoism and the pure pursuit of profit idea.

You may be wondering: How do we get there from here? More specifically, how do we persuade people who believe otherwise that capitalism is not, or certainly need not be, a dog-eat-dog system?

In this chapter, I discuss an important development within the business world that, if it were more widely known and more widely put into practice, would help greatly to reinforce the moral dimension of capitalism as understood along the lines of NDC, and as explained in the previous chapter. I am referring to a movement within the field of business management that has been underway for more than half a century.

A Revolution In Business Management

The movement to which I am referring has gone by a number of different names—the Quality Movement, Total Quality Management, the Quality Imperative, the Democratization of the Workplace, the Re-Engineering of Business. I have my own name for this movement: "Quality and Ethics Management," or QEM. The essence of QEM is the idea that treating people respectfully in business is almost always best from a strictly profit-oriented point of view, and of course is the right thing to do anyway. *My book A Good Day's work: Sustaining Ethical Behavior and Business* Success (coauthored with Alice Darnell Lattal, and published in 2007), discusses some of the history and applications of this idea. It is such an important idea that it deserves to be described as revolutionary.

The Japanese began the revolution in the early 1950s when they adopted the views of two American consultants, W. Edwards Deming and Joseph M. Juran. Deming became known for asking such questions as these: Are people at work rewarded for success rather than being punished for failure? Are they routinely asked for their opinions on how best to do their jobs? Are they treated as though they were bona fide members of a "corporate family" or business partnership that provides them with a stake in the success of the company for which they work? Are loyal employees made to feel secure in their jobs, insofar as the economic situation of a company makes this possible?

The ideas of Deming and Juran were rediscovered in America and Europe in the 1980s and began to spread around the world. More recent management theories combine the work of Deming and Juran with that of Kaoru Ishikawa and other pioneers in Japan, and with a growing body of literature from many nations on effective management and leadership techniques.

Core Concepts Of QEM

While QEM is not a wholly unified movement, the following two core ideas stand out:

> * Success in business is a function of systems more than anything else. An individual business is a complex system that integrates such elements as design, manufacturing, marketing, and service. A system that contains the best incentives for everyone to do their jobs well and to improve the system itself will be the most successful in the long run.

> * The most important dimension of a good business system is its positive treatment of people in it and affected by it—customers, employees, consultants, suppliers, investors, community members, and others.

In large part because of the QEM movement, advocates of strong, positive moral values can now easily find common cause with business managers who might in the past have had more strictly profit-oriented reasons for wanting to treat people well. The principles of Universal Moral Pluralism, discussed in Chapter 8, have a much better chance of being integrated into the world of business because of QEM. People can feel reassured that the moral dimension of NDC is realistic. They can feel reassured that capitalism really is a good thing.

Allow me to spell out in some detail the points that I have just made.

Successful companies must treat consumers well in order to keep them as loyal customers. The Japanese discovered the full significance of this fact earlier than Americans did. More than differing wage scales in earlier decades or differing cultural attitudes, this discovery was the reason why Japanese automobiles and electronics gained world predominance in the 1980s. Because of the emerging global economy, "captive markets" within countries, or regions of countries, were disappearing even then for numerous consumer products and services, which meant that the larger scope of global competition was strengthening incentives for companies to treat customers well. At the present time, only companies whose customers absolutely must buy locally can afford not to treat those customers well, because otherwise people can buy what they want somewhere else where they are treated better.

Consumers have always wanted to buy products and services from businesses that treat their customers well not simply in order to make profits, but instead treat people well for the sake of doing the right thing. These are companies that *genuinely* promote consumers' interests under all circumstances. Although it may seem paradoxical, companies that operate in this manner are the ones most likely to make profits in the long run, since one of the most valuable business assets that a company can possess is a willingness to do what is right regardless of expected profit. Behaving in such a way is the essence of moral integrity in business. Let me repeat: One of the most valuable business assets that any company can possess is a willingness to do what is right regardless of expected profit.

Successful companies must treat employees and suppliers well in order to maintain their loyalty. They must also treat investors well. Talented and hard working individuals have always wanted to work for companies that genuinely value their employees, in contrast to companies that treat workers well during the good times and then discard them quickly during a downturn in the economy. For their part, successful companies have a strong economic incentive to treat employees well in order to keep them long-term as loyal workers, especially in today's high-tech industries where extensive employee training represents a substantial investment for corporations. For all types of businesses, whenever employees leave a company they take their skills and knowledge of the company with them. Effective strategies for maintaining a loyal work force include making workplaces more democratic and giving workers a genuine financial stake in the success of the company, either through salary increases or bonuses tied to company profits or through employee stock ownership.

Just as with their employees, successful companies need the full cooperation of their suppliers. The "on-time" inventory systems pioneered by Japanese companies require a cordial and trusting relationship between a manufacturer and its numerous suppliers of components and materials, in order to ensure that deliveries of components and materials are consistently made at just the right times and in just the right quantities. Increased global competition and the fast pace of technological change mean that companies need the same trusting relationship with investors, because when a company begins to lose ground there is often a need for immediate access to capital for necessary improvements in the company's operations.

Successful companies need the goodwill of successful people in the communities where they manufacture products. Everything from the control of vandalism on company property to adequate fire protection and good schools and hospitals for employees depends on the goodwill of people in the community. Successful companies depend upon good local governments that strongly support these companies because the companies are known to be good "community citizens."

In short, a new commandment now exists for business managers: Treat everyone well. Of course, this commandment does not automatically apply to every company as regards the bottom line, and some types of companies more than others need to heed this commandment in order to be profitable. The companies that can most afford to *ignore* this commandment are ones protected by government from competition.

Some managers at the present time continue to ignore this commandment simply because they do not understand its significance.

Moving Beyond Authoritarian Management

Too many companies are still being run according to old-fashioned authoritarian management philosophies that encourage the use of fear as a management technique. "Sales staff must meet their monthly quotas—or else." Of course, sometimes managers do need to take a hard line. But just as often, managers who make hard-line statements ignore factors that are beyond the control of employees, who then live in perpetual fear. Until the end of his long life, W. Edwards Deming continued to teach that fear must be banished from the workplace. Where it is not, he said, not only do employees suffer because their individuality is not respected, but so also does the corporate bottom line because management is not able to elicit from workers their best performance. (A good source for Deming's ideas is his *Out of the Crisis*, published in 1986. See especially Chapter 3 for his discussion of fear in the workplace.)

In the past, corporate executives who believed—or said they believed—in the superiority of an essentially free market economy often failed to see that they had created *within their own companies* an authoritarian structure where individual employees were subjected to heavy-handed control. QEM insists that this situation be remedied. The primary remedy is for managers to tell employees what the company wants from them—excellent products, satisfied customers, innovative ideas for improving competitiveness—and then allow employ-

126

ees to figure out for themselves many of the details of how best to obtain these results.

Along the way, managers must articulate the company's overall goals and values in the form of a corporate philosophy, or set of comprehensive corporate goals, that respects individuality. If employees are treated as mere cogs in a wheel, they will not contribute as genuine team members. They will be harmed and the company will be harmed.

One way to help inform employees about a company's goals is to train them in more than one area, a practice encouraged by QEM. An emphasis on training of many different kinds is a cornerstone of Deming's teachings. The basic insight is simplicity itself: Workers will do a better job if they have full knowledge of what they are doing. Beyond that, if employees are trained to do more than a single job within an organization, they will more likely feel themselves to be an integral part of the company. Such "cross training" provides employees with greater information about the company as a whole which, moreover, is hands-on information that cannot be put into an instruction manual. Such training also provides a cushion in case a particular department or division is scaled back or closed down, because employees are already trained for other positions than the ones they occupy, and it also happens sometimes that when an employee is trained for a new job, the employee discovers that she has greater aptitude for the new job than for the old one. The employee is a better fit in the new job. Training for a number of different jobs also tends to make life at work more interesting for employees.

Less Competition Within Companies

Another important feature of QEM is its commitment to corporate structures that place less emphasis than in the past on competition *within* companies. While there is nothing wrong with the general idea of competition within a company, it is the potential for such competition more than actual competition that encourages workers to be productive. Within and between departments of the same company, cooperation is more important than competition—and also is more likely to make life enjoyable for the people engaged in it. There is also the redundancy factor when several different teams are told to work on a new product design or marketing strategy, where the work of only one of these teams will be used in the end. By contrast, while competition for the highest quarterly sales numbers does not produce redundant efforts, it does often have a different sort of bad consequence: It tends to undermine the feeling among employees that "we are all in this together" working to make the company successful.

An ironic fact about the business world is that old-fashioned authoritarian companies resemble planned, socialistic economies too much in one respect—through having rigid, top-down management practices—but sometimes resemble free markets too much in another respect, by fostering excessive competition within the organization itself. It is much better for managers to commit themselves to the idea that most employees just naturally want to do a good job, and do not usually require the sort of pressure that comes from having a lot of competition within a company.

The Increased Scope Of Global Competition

Is it possible for competition to be reduced within a company, even while the scope of competition increases around the world within a global economy?

Critics of the global economy and capitalism complain that

soon the entire world will be permeated by "cut-throat competition." These critics are promoting a variation on a complaint that has been made numerous times on a smaller scale during the past two centuries and more. This complaint is no more true now than it ever was.

The truth is that free markets *permit* a lot of actual competition but do not require it, either within companies, within society at large, or around the world. Under capitalism, people are free to compete with one another but equally are free to join together in voluntary associations whose purpose is to lessen or eliminate competition among members. People are free to join any existing organization that will accept them, and everyone is free to experiment with new forms of cooperation both within the business world and outside it. People may wish to create nonprofit business ventures or enter into friendships, partnerships, or other personal associations that shield them from competition. People are free to join labor unions and to bargain for employment policies that lessen competition among employees. Owners of businesses can choose to offer long-term contracts to employees for the purpose of strengthening employee loyalty or for any other reason deemed economically sound. Longer term contracts, in conjunction with seniority benefits that make jobs more secure, can reduce drastically the extent of day-to-day competitive pressures at work. More of an employee's energy can go toward working effectively and enjoying life.

A Pleasant Workplace Environment

QEM decrees that the number one job of management is to design the overall business system in such a way as to insure that employees are confronted every day with incentives that encourage them to cooperate with one another and with management. A good place for management to begin is by making

129

the workplace as pleasant an environment as possible. Desks, lighting, chairs, anti-glare computer screens, control of noise levels and distractions in an office or factory—all are important. So also is an understanding that no one can work continuously for long periods of time with a complete focus on the job and still maintain a high level of efficiency. For many types of jobs, a certain amount of friendly conversation, banter, and "catching up" among workers on the job, if not excessive, can improve efficiency and also help to promote the feeling that being at work is like being with family members. (There are exceptional types of jobs, of course, such as air traffic control, where a complete focus on the job is extremely important.) Another important area is compliance with company rules: Just as high compliance costs for meeting cumbersome government regulations undermine a *company's* overall efficiency and profitability, cumbersome procedures for reporting job performance and other personnel matters undermine an *employee's* efficiency and enjoyment at work.

Workers who are treated with consideration day-in-and-day-out and who enjoy their jobs have all the more reason to want to be at work and to do a good job. Incentives at work, when a company is managed well, continually reinforce a worker's good feelings and positive outlook. Because most people devote the largest single block of time in their lives to activities involving work, the degree of satisfaction, or lack of satisfaction, in a person's work life is a major contributor to that person's happiness or unhappiness. Good managers want their employees to be happy both for the company's sake and for the employees' sake.

Moreover, good feelings, whenever and wherever they occur, are contagious, containing a multiplier effect that is all the more likely to make a real difference in the workplace if employees perceive that they will still be treated well regardless of the company's quarterly profits. This perception will in all likelihood lead workers to be more productive and to *increase* quarterly profits.

Independence And Team Spirit

A related idea that may appear paradoxical, but really is not, is that allowing workers on the job more independence will increase their team spirit, besides being the morally right thing to do in any case. An employee who is required to follow rigid, unpleasant work rules with no opportunity to make changes in his or her daily regimen will spend a lot of time at work thinking about personal issues, such as how to make it through the day with as little pain as possible, how to cut corners and get away with doing so, or how to take steps that will lead to obtaining another job. Such an employee encounters numerous incentives during the course of a typical day at work that yield negative outcomes both for the employee and for the company. By contrast, an employee who is allowed more independence will be able to decide for himself how he can contribute most effectively to team efforts in the workplace. He will not spend a large portion of his day thinking about how to escape from his present workplace situation.

After all, what does motivate individuals or teams of individuals at work to do a good job? The most important answer is this: Because there is nothing else to do.

I do not mean this to be a frivolous answer.

There is nothing else to do at work except a good job *unless impediments are placed in the way.* As Deming and others have emphasized, the motivation to do a good job is a given for most employees; it is an internal incentive that exists as a kind of default setting within the minds of most people. For most people, pride in a job well done plays an important role in making life meaningful. If doing a good job requires team effort, as it almost always does at least to some extent, then workers will "just naturally" be motivated to work effectively as team members unless contrary motivators are built into the system. Doing a bad job is very frequently a reaction to negative circumstances: inadequate training, an unpleasant work environment, authoritarian management, unfair hiring or promotion policies, or illogical procedures in the office or on the factory floor.

Autonomy In The Workplace

Autonomy means "being one's own person." An autonomous individual possesses opportunities to make a broad range of choices that affect his or her life in important ways. Some of the harshest critics of capitalism say that capitalism destroys autonomy because most people must work for a living, and everyone who is employed within a market economy is rigidly controlled by a system of financial rewards and punishments. The owners and managers of companies possess all the real power, say these critics, who then ask: How can I be my own person when someone else is telling me how to do my job, and when my choices among jobs, or between employment and unemployment, are determined by economic factors over which I have no control?

However, autonomy is a type of freedom, and as everyone knows, freedom can be and often is misused. The very idea of being free entails being *able* to do both what is acceptable and what is not acceptable within one's society or within one's place of employment. As a consequence, freedom as a societal value involves what is sometimes called the "paradox of freedom":

Unless the freedom of certain individuals is curtailed, the freedom of others will be jeopardized. This alleged paradox applies as much in the world of business as anywhere else. In the workplace, some individuals are inevitably going to be disruptive, uncooperative, or ineffective; their behavior is a threat to the freedom of other individuals to do their jobs properly. Disruptive and uncooperative individuals in the workplace undermine the autonomy of everyone else.

Therefore, one of the crucial functions of a good manager is to establish rules and guidelines essential to the general respect for autonomy: Showing up for work on time (which may involve any number of different "flex-time" arrangements), completing work on schedule, being courteous to customers and one's fellow workers. Employees who follow the basic rules are rewarded, those who don't are not rewarded. Setting limits to freedom for the sake of autonomy is not inconsistent for the simple reason that "complete freedom means no freedom at all."

At the same time, workplace autonomy *is* undermined when a manager enforces arbitrary or authoritarian rules and procedures, or when an employer emphasizes punishing failure rather than rewarding success. Then an employee does truly feel like a puppet on a string. However, autonomy is not the only thing jeopardized when this happens. So also is profitability, because an employee who does not feel that he is his own person will not work to his full potential.

Let me repeat: Workplaces that emphasize punishing failure rather than rewarding success are threats to autonomy, but such workplaces are also threats to the success of the company. To use the language of psychology: Good managers are the ones who have learned to rely primarily on *positive reinforcement* within the workplace. They have learned to minimize negative reinforcement and punishment. This is one of the most important lessons belonging to the QEM movement. (A discussion of positive reinforcement, negative reinforcement, punishment, and how they can best be used in the workplace, is to be found in *A Good Day's Work*, mentioned above, especially Chapter 15.)

It is important to keep in mind as well that free market economics goes hand in hand with the protection of freedom and basic rights that are essential to autonomy in all areas of life. More than any other economic or political system, capitalism allows people the freedom to change jobs, train for new jobs, start their own companies, and spend their money as they wish. The economic successes of strongly capitalistic societies, in creating more and better jobs, improve workplace opportunities and thereby strengthen autonomy.

The QEM movement is helping to make workplaces more democratic and work more pleasant and meaningful. QEM is making it easier for advocates of strong, positive moral values to find common cause with business managers who always had—but did not always know that they had—more strictly profit-oriented reasons for wanting to treat people well. It is much easier now than in past decades (not to mention past centuries!) for advocates of capitalistic government to find common cause with crusaders for higher moral standards in business.

Nevertheless, many people continue to believe that capitalism is inherently immoral. In the next chapter, I provide additional reasons for rejecting this claim.

Chapter 10.
The Closing of Factories under Capitalism

As numerous critics of capitalism see it, the issue of factory closings illustrates the existence of an unavoidable confrontation between capitalism and morality. Capitalism "dictates" that an unprofitable or marginally profitable factory be closed regardless of the human costs, while a concern for morality dictates that a factory be kept open except in extreme cases even if this means a loss of profits. The factory should be kept open to ensure that the essential needs of employees and community members continue to be met.

Who Is To Blame?

In the minds of many people, particularly those who are themselves hurt by the shutdown of a large factory, there exists an impersonal system—capitalism—that has them in its grip. The system is perpetuated by a small number of individuals in positions of power who care nothing about the needs of employees or the good of society. Because a global economy tends to give even greater power to these individuals, the situation has continued to get worse in recent years, according to many of the critics of capitalism. Therefore, they say, while government interventions in economic matters have always been necessary to make up for the "inadequacies of capitalism," interventions are now needed all the more within the context of a global economy.

However, if what I say in earlier chapters is correct, no confrontation exists between capitalism and morality. A confrontation may exist between an individual factory manager and the people affected by a proposed shutdown. But if capitalism is the best economic system, then it is unfair to blame capitalism for problems created by the shutdown of a particular factory. The people to blame are those involved in the closing itself if they have not handled the situation in the best way: managers of the company if they have not done enough to make the factory profitable and are not doing enough to help displaced employees; the board of directors of the corporation if they have made mistakes; labor leaders if their policies have been anticompetitive; or the employees themselves if they could reasonably have done their jobs more effectively in order to keep the factory profitable. At the present time, because we live under a mixed economy that contains large non-capitalistic elements, the largest share of blame when a factory closes may lie with government for over-taxing the business and subjecting it to high compliance costs in meeting complex regulations.

Responsibilities Of Management

Let us ask the following question: What if the managers and board of directors do not bear much responsibility for the economic predicament of a factory that is not doing well? Let us suppose that all of these people have done their jobs as well as can reasonably be expected in their efforts to keep the factory profitable. What, then, is the responsibility of management when a decision is being considered to close a factory for pressing economic reasons?

For NDC, these individuals have important moral obligations to employees and community members that are in addition to their obligations to stockholders. These moral obligations include the following:

* To notify employees about the closing as soon as possible;
* To make no false or misleading statements about the likelihood of reopening the factory;
* To make every effort to rehire displaced workers at other facilities, including retraining them if necessary for new jobs.

In a typical case where a large manufacturing facility is about to be closed, a great many of the workers will have been employed there during a significant part of their lives. They will have friends at work and homes in the community. For many of them, spouses will have jobs in the area and their children will attend local schools. Only a few of these families will be able to move easily if that becomes necessary. If the factory has played a major role in the economy of the area, then its closing will mean the loss of numerous support jobs and a decline in the tax base with resulting shortages for schools, police, hospitals, etc. Property values will drop. In the worst sorts of cases, people who have spent a lifetime working to increase the value of commercial or residential property may take large losses.

None of this means that a factory ought to be kept open at all costs, because the obligation to help people in need must be balanced against other moral obligations. It does mean that sometimes a factory should be kept open longer than a strict consideration of profitability would dictate—if (and only if) the company can afford to keep it open. It means that a man-

137

ager who is sensitive to the repercussions of closing a factory will, before making the final decision, take into consideration all of the obvious and not-so-obvious human hardships that would result from a shutdown. Then if the factory is closed, steps will be taken to help displaced workers and the community. Advanced notice will be given of the closing if that is feasible.

Do managers always take their moral responsibilities seriously in such cases? Of course they do not. Many things can go wrong, including the way that managers perceive their exercise of power.

Exercising Legitimate Power

One of the more disconcerting facts about human nature is how quickly people become accustomed to wielding power once they acquire it. As the exercise of power becomes second nature to people in positions of authority, in business and elsewhere, it is easy for these people to become insensitive to the consequences upon others that their exercise of power may have. Executives of large corporations have a special need to remind themselves of this, especially when they are in the midst of deciding whether or not to close a factory. The immediate bases for the decision to close a factory—quarterly reports, market projections, information about competitors, assessments of tax liabilities, etc.—will be readily available on the executive's desk or computer screen, while the hardships suffered by laid-off workers and their communities will exist at a distance.

Corporate executives should remind themselves that the exercise of *legitimate* power can be dangerous because, for one reason, it is likely to produce complacency both in those who wield it and in those who are affected by it. Most executives have risen to positions of authority as the result of talent and hard work, so it is understandable that many of these individuals feel that they deserve to exercise great power. This feeling may blind them to their moral responsibilities, which include helping people in need and doing their part to make society a better place.

Fortunately, much more is being said and done these days than ever before to remind people in the business world of their moral obligations. There are numerous articles in business journals and ethics journals, seminars for executives, required ethics courses for business students in college, and an increasing amount of media attention paid to ethical issues in both business and politics. We as a society in the United States are on the right track overall, and the same is true for other advanced countries. I believe that the ideas and ideals that belong to NDC and QEM can help a lot to ensure that business managers and directors stay on the right track and strengthen their ethical commitments. These ideas and ideals provide a perspective from which society can justly criticize managers and directors who do not fulfill their moral responsibilities.

This last point is especially important. Citizens and voters who are informed about the economic, political, psychological, and moral dimensions of capitalism as I spell them out in this book will be in a strong position to publically criticize business and government leaders who do not fulfill their moral responsibilities. The "will of the people," if well-informed and sufficiently unified, can be an immensely powerful force for good. The key is for citizens and voters to be informed about the economic strengths of capitalism and the moral responsibilities of people in business and government.

Laws That Dictate Social Responsibilities

Opponents of capitalistic government are not content with

moral criticism of managers who neglect their responsibilities when a factory is closed. These opponents want laws that *dictate* the social responsibilities of managers in situations such as when a factory is about to close. In some cases, say these critics of capitalism, government should prohibit factories from closing in order to keep individuals and communities from being hurt by the shutdown.

The first point that I want to make in response to these critics is that when laws are passed that lessen or remove the power of executives to decide when and how to close factories, the executives lose opportunities to learn more about how to assess factory closings from a comprehensive moral perspective such as I describe in Chapter 8. The incentives brought into existence by laws that dictate morality in business are all wrong because they exempt executives from having to make the hard moral choices. Instead, executives end up being motivated primarily to do whatever they can to lessen financial loses to their companies while complying with the laws. No genuine moral consciousness-raising is likely to result.

My second point is that, from an economic point of view, laws that dictate the social responsibilities of management are objectionable because they are inconsistent with essential free market principles. They restrict economic freedom while increasing the coercive powers of government. They increase the already huge compliance burden on businesses.

Consider laws that require factory managers to give 60 days notice to employees before a factory is closed. Such laws ignore the fact that sometimes it is necessary to close a factory on much shorter notice than this. Many factors are at work: the fast pace of technological change, shifting populations, the realization that smaller work groups are sometimes more effectively managed than larger groups, and the emergence of new markets. Businesses must become more flexible, not less flexible, in responding to global market realities.

Also, laws that require advance notice of factory closings are inherently arbitrary. Who can say in general how much notice should be given? One month? Two months? Three months? Who can say what is best even for the "typical" case, let alone the exceptional case? And even if we could somehow know that in most instances giving 60 days notice was the "best all-around policy," this would not justify passing a law requiring that two months notice be given in every case. Exceptional cases would be ignored by such a law, which means that over the long run the law would likely penalize some of the most innovative companies.

On the other hand, if various types of exceptional circumstances are built into factory-closings laws, which is true for actual laws presently on the books in the U.S., then increases in the sizes of government agencies are required for implementation. The exact sizes, staffing levels, and budgets of such agencies must be arrived at in a laborious fashion, because that is the way that government works. The policies and deliberations of such agencies will likely be years behind the true needs of business, because that again is the way that government works. The business world is highly complex, highly integrated, and subject to rapid systems-wide changes, while legislative processes under the best of circumstances are highly cumbersome. Therefore, it is inevitable that government controls of every sort will function with a heavy hand and ignore the special needs of individual cases, regardless of how fine-tuned government regulations are. In fact, fine-tuning often makes matters worse because it requires larger and more unwieldy bureaucracies and higher compliance costs.

Government by its very nature tends to be inflexible and

ponderous, which brings stability and security to the protection of basic rights. Protecting basic rights is government at its best, doing something extremely important that government is uniquely qualified to do. But if government takes on the role of legislating common decency in the world of business, it ties itself into a kind of gigantic knot. As a matter of principle, government should not be assigned the job of legislating common decency.

HELP FOR DISPLACED WORKERS

Some people say that when a factory closes, government has a moral obligation to hire displaced workers or train them for new jobs. The obvious question to ask is where the money will come from to pay for government hiring or training programs. The number one question always is: What must be sacrificed elsewhere in the economy—now or in the future—in order to pay for a proposed government program? (This is the question raised in Chapter 7 under the heading of "what might have been.") Regrettably, this question is usually not asked by politicians, bureaucrats, or news reporters, who either have reasons for pretending *not* to have thought of the question or else are ignorant of the underlying economic principles.

Moreover, when government appropriates money for a jobs training program or for anything else, it does not simply transfer money from the private sector where the money could have contributed to employment in some form. A considerable portion of the money is lost in the process of transfer because the wheels of government turn expensively and ponderously even when no corruption is present. A net decrease—now or in the future—in money available for payrolls, facilities, materials, and training is inevitable.

Of course, exceptional situations are possible where a par-

142

ticular government-funded program happens to be well run, or where it anticipates the needs of consumers or industry better than people in the private sector are doing. Many highly competent and dedicated people work for government, so it is always possible that a public sector undertaking can outperform a similar effort in the private sector, despite the fact that the types of incentives belonging to the private sector are on the whole far superior to the types of incentives belonging to the public sector as regards "getting the job done" in training workers or increasing employment opportunities. Sometimes stimulus money from the government does provide a very helpful boost to the economy of a region where jobs are being lost. But even if a particular government employment program does work well, this does not mean that the next government employment program will be equally effective, or effective at all. It does not mean that the degree of power granted to government to enable it to run employment programs is desirable. Most government programs regardless of purpose are initiated by legislators who are subject to strong pressures to serve the interests of their constituents, or those among their constituents who are most visible, aggressive, or generous in giving campaign contributions. Whether legislators themselves are moral or not-so-moral, they must please the people whose support they need at election time. If government is given the power to create employment programs this year, it will possess that power for many years to come. The power will be used and abused in numerous ways. It will be extended into other areas.

Another question: Is there any reason to believe that government employment training programs will produce the kinds of skills that industry actually needs in order to provide more good jobs? Most such training programs in the past have been geared toward teaching relatively low level skills, not the highly technical ones that are required for the U.S. to improve its competitiveness against global competition. Can government improve its efforts in this area by putting more emphasis on highly technical jobs training?

Not really. The problem is that "highly technical jobs training" means a thousand different things in the fast changing world of high tech industries. Can government choose from among all the options the best areas for technical training? Again, the only realistic answer is no. Regardless of how well-intentioned government efforts are, they will always, overall, lag behind the cutting edge in industry because of the nature of the political process, and this is especially true in regard to the highly complex technologies that drive the global economy.

Government Bailouts

Should a corporation seek or accept a government subsidy in order to avoid closing a factory, especially when the shutdown will likely cause much hardship? Suppose that the company has no choice but to close the factory unless it receives a government bailout.

In the years immediately prior to 2008, many supporters of the idea that giving government bailouts to struggling companies is a good thing pointed to the example of Chrysler Corporation. Their argument was that the Chrysler Corporation Loan Guarantee Act, which became law in 1980 at a time when Chrysler was struggling, not only allowed Chrysler to borrow enough money to stay in business but enabled Chrysler to regroup and redesign its cars so as to be able to offer American consumers appealing choices in the marketplace that they otherwise would not have had. In fact, Chrysler did bounce back to become a strong, innovative corporation for a few years, offering consumers some excellent choices, and providing good jobs to its employees. Chrysler paid back all of the guaranteed loans ahead of time. All of these events took place before Chrysler became part of DaimlerChrysler in 1998, and well before the subsequent decline in profitability for the Chrysler arm of DaimlerChrysler. A case can be made that the management of DaimlerChrysler (now Daimler AG) made a huge mistake when they removed most members of the highly effective management team in place at Chrysler in 1998. At any event, Chrysler was sold by DaimlerChrysler at a loss in 2007 to Cerberus Capital Management, but continued to struggle and soon needed help once again. As of 2009, Chrysler had received approximately $7 billion from the federal government.

What if Chrysler had not become a part of DaimlerChrysler in 1998, had weathered the economic downturn of 2008, and had continued indefinitely to be a successful automaker? Could we then say that the Chrysler loan guarantees of 1980 were a good thing? The answer is *no*. Even if an individual situation involving a government bailout may appear to yield more benefits than harms, government subsidies, loans, or loan guarantees are a bad *kind* of aid because they extend the powers of government further than those powers ought to be extended. The question of "what might have been" is unavoidable since money given out in one area by government necessarily is taken from somewhere else in the economy. If all that government does is guarantee a loan from a private source (and thus does not actually spend any money), it is still true that the money loaned from this source would otherwise have gone somewhere else, and if the company that is bailed out eventually defaults on the guaranteed loan then the government will be required to pay out the money directly, which once again will reduce the amount of money available elsewhere in the economy. Inevitably, whenever government attempts to help businesses financially, it robs Peter to pay Paul, and in the process is subject to all of the inefficiencies and corruptive pressures that exist within large governmental structures.

Business executives themselves share much of the blame for promoting the idea that government should bail out companies that are in trouble. Chrysler Corporation campaigned vigorously for help back in 1980. In actuality, the main beneficiaries of bailouts are the executives who get to hold onto their jobs and the politicians who get support from people in their districts for "saving jobs." The executives and politicians in such cases usually try to convince voters that when a company goes bankrupt, it disappears from existence like Cinderella's coach at midnight, taking all of its jobs and facilities with it, never to return. Therefore a bailout does an immense amount of good, they say, in stopping all of this from happening. The reality is quite different, however. Typically, when a company goes bankrupt the company's facilities and assets merely change hands. They are not lost. It is true that many people may lose jobs when a factory closes or a company goes through bankruptcy proceedings, but after the dust settles someone usually gets a chance to run the company or the factory on better financial terms, or at least to use its assets in some new ways—and often in ways that provide better jobs in the long run. The process of "creative destruction," as its name implies, does involve something negative—the destruction of the old company or the old factory—but also something positive when new uses are found for existing assets. Occasionally, a factory does close for good, the buildings are torn down, the land remains vacant, and little can be done to use any of the equipment left behind. Employees and the local economy may then take a large hit. But this happens only when a factory and its equipment are already out of date or in poor condition. Such a factory is way past saving economically by any means.

If government subsidy programs are already in place and competitors are taking advantage of them, it is understandable that the CEO of a company will attempt to obtain a subsidy in order to avoid closing a factory, particularly if the refusal to seek the subsidy would be seen as an empty gesture and the factory closing would be seen as a black mark against the corporation. But this does not make the subsidy program correct as a matter of principle.

The Only Exception

There is an exceptional type of situation where a government bailout *can be* justified. It is the only such exception. Large financial lending institutions that are closely linked to the Federal Reserve may sometimes properly be judged "too large to fail" in the event of a severe economic downturn such as the one that began in 2008.

There are two important reasons why the federal government via the Treasury Department and the Federal Reserve was justified in coming to the aid of lending institutions in 2008. The first is that the financial crisis involving these institutions was to a large extent caused by actions of the federal government, as I explained in Chapter 4. A lot of pressure was put on Fannie and Freddie going back to the Clinton administration that strongly encouraged the granting of loans to individuals who failed to meet long-established criteria for being creditworthy. In addition, long-established rules for the capitalization of banks were changed for Fannie Mae and Freddie Mac, allowing them to play a much riskier lending game than had previously been allowed.

The second reason is that the economy of the U.S. as a whole, indeed the economy of the world, was put at risk by the drying up of credit that accompanied the initial mortgage crisis. Numerous businesses around the world, through no fault of their own, were suddenly and severely jeopardized. Among the hardest hit were auto companies, both domestic and foreign, which require for their survival that auto buyers be able to get credit for new car purchases, for the obvious reason that buying a new car takes a large bite out of most families' budgets. For most people, borrowing a substantial amount of money is an absolute requirement when they buy a new car. Since the fault *did lie* to a large extent with the federal government, and since only the federal government had the power and wherewithal to intervene quickly and effectively, the responsibility for taking the initial steps to set things right belonged to the federal government. But that is where government interventions should have stopped. The Federal government should not have made billions of dollars available to Chrysler, GM, and other large companies.

Let us return to the discussion of factory closings.

Causes Of Factory Closings

Numerous plant closings in the Unites States in recent years could have been avoided if people had acted correctly on matters of principle at an earlier time.

Management failure. Consider the steel industry. Many observers agree that one of the main causes of the decline in the American steel industry during the 1970s and 1980s, which resulted in numerous mill closings, was management failure to stand firm against union demands that ultimately contributed to making American steel uncompetitive against foreign steel. Wages were pushed above market levels. Yet, many people then

148

and now see the conflict between the United Steel Workers and management as involving another dimension of the supposed "classic confrontation" between capitalism and morality. This is not the best way to view the situation.

A brief look at the history of American labor/management relations will help to provide a better perspective.

In the early years of the twentieth century when large corporations, for example some that were engaged in coal mining in West Virginia, routinely violated the rights of workers to organize themselves and gain a degree of autonomy, the solution was judged to lie in policies that gave organized labor more power in order to be in a better position to oppose the power of big business. Doing this did make sense at the time, but it was not the best response for the long term. What should have been done was to curtail the existing de facto power of business that was being used—often with the collusion of state or local governments—to violate the rights of workers, such as happened in the events leading up to the Matewan Massacre in 1920 in West Virginia and the ensuing Battle of Blair Mountain in 1921. Management/labor issues early in the twentieth century were seen essentially in terms of a power struggle between owners, on the one hand, and workers, on the other hand, where the latter were judged to possess too little power, which was unquestionably true. But just as important, more should have been done to define more clearly, and protect much more vigorously, the basic rights of workers to organize and to speak out against unfair management practices.

Protectionist legislation. Another cause for present day factory closings in America is protectionist legislation that shortsighted individuals advocate as a solution to the problem of declining profitability resulting from foreign competition. Again, the issue is often seen as another dimension of the supposed confrontation between capitalism and morality. Advocates of protectionist legislation claim that there is a moral need to protect workers against foreign competition. However, the result of protectionist legislation is the exact opposite of what is desired: Not stronger domestic industries—where jobs are more secure—but weaker industries that are even less able to compete in world markets, and where more jobs are inevitably lost over the longer term.

It is an inescapable fact that foreign competition strengthens every company that is economically salvageable by subjecting it to day-in-and-day-out pressures that force the company to improve. The underlying psychological principle is simplicity itself: The best business and workplace decisions overall get made in the best motivational context. A protectionist industrial policy on the part of the federal government provides managers with strong incentives to make their companies eligible for protection, and not necessarily to do their best to meet competition. As a consequence, companies end up being *less effective* competitors, and therefore more in need of protectionist help; the situation spirals downhill. Inevitably, there are ripple effects throughout a company from its posture in the market: If the hidden or not-so-hidden message to employees is to do things in the old way because the old way is protected by government, a hundred different choices will be made each day by design, production, and sales staff to reinforce the old way. Incentives throughout the company will become skewed in unintended directions that yield unwanted consequences. But if the pressures faced every day are the make-it-or-break-it pressures that originate from the presence of highly skilled competitors in the marketplace, at home or abroad, then all across the company people will be doing their best to improve the company's performance in both large and small ways in order to meet the competition.

Once Again, Capitalism And Morality

There is a lesson to be learned from the efforts of government to protect businesses and workers on moral grounds against the supposed evils, or at least the supposed moral indifference, of capitalism in connection with the closing of factories. The lesson is that the supposed confrontation between capitalism and morality is misconceived, and government's efforts based on this misconception are usually counterproductive. The entire reactive enterprise on the part of government is usually a hindrance to realizing genuine moral reform in the world of business. This is true regardless of the particular area where the supposed confrontation is said to exist—factory closings, labor/management issues, protectionism, bailouts, and many others.

Chapter 11.
Low Taxes, West Virginia

In this chapter, I discuss the first part of my proposed slogan for the state of West Virginia: **Low Taxes, Least Red Tape, Highest Ethics**. The number one goal of any state in competition with other states should be to minimize all taxes that impose penalties on success in running a business, being employed by a business, or investing in a business. Let us make Low Taxes, West Virginia a reality as soon as possible.

Above All Else, Reduce Taxes

As I finish writing this book in 2010, it is becoming clear that Governor Manchin, who recently left office in the middle of his second term to become a U.S. senator, has been more successful than any previous governor in improving the economic climate of West Virginia. Manchin's successes have had to do primarily with reducing business-oriented taxes. An initial step in the right direction was taken in 1999 when Governor Cecil Underwood initiated the Commission on Fair Taxation. Little was accomplished before Underwood's single term in office ended in 2000 (Underwood had also served as governor of

West Virginia many years earlier), nor was much accomplished to reduce taxes during the single term of Governor Bob Wise, who succeeded Underwood. Manchin took office in 2004, and in 2005 established the Tax Modernization Project, which has resulted in substantial tax reforms.

In part, these reforms reflect the views of Russell Sobel, whose book, *Unleashing Capitalism: Why Prosperity Stops at the West Virginia Border and How to Fix It*, was published in 2007. Sobel is the primary editor of Unleashing Capitalism and also is the coauthor of several chapters in the book. Soon after the book was published, Sobel was invited to present his case for improving West Virginia's economy to Governor Manchin. *Unleashing Capitalism* contains recommendations for tax reforms in four areas: Reducing the rate of the state corporate income tax; repealing the state's personal property tax on inventory, machinery, and equipment owned by businesses; repealing West Virginia's business franchise tax; and phasing out business tax credits.

Reducing taxes is an important part of what West Virginia must do in order to become the country's most business-friendly state. In today's world, where consumers in most countries have access to goods produced around the globe, there is no room for tax policies that weaken a state's competitive position because even a small difference in competitiveness can make a huge difference in the profitability of a state's businesses. Who wants to buy a consumer item from West Virginia for $10.00 when an item of the same quality is available for $9.75 from another state or country that is just a little bit more business-friendly? Competition for sales applies to consumers both within and outside the United States. It is in the interest of West Virginia to maximize its share of the American export market as well as its share of the domestic market.

The same reasoning that applies to West Virginia's competitiveness in regard to selling its products and services applies as well to the competition that our state faces to attract and hold onto the "best and the brightest." In today's world, the people who have the most to offer to a society can, to a large extent, go where they choose and take their talents, money, energy, and companies with them. Thus, governments and social systems at all levels face increasing external pressures to take steps toward instituting reforms, especially in the direction of lowering taxes. Our number one task in West Virginia is to respond to these pressures in the most effective way.

The Corporate Net Income Tax

In early 2006, the top rate for West Virginia's corporate net income tax was 9%, which meant that West Virginia had the seventh highest such rate in the U.S. It should be obvious that anyone considering whether to locate a business in West Virginia, or expand an existing business, will pay a lot of attention to the corporate net income tax rate. West Virginia's high rate has long been a major obstacle to business growth within the state. But business growth is what the state needs more than anything else in order to strengthen competition among companies for employees within West Virginia who will be added to the payrolls of the state's businesses. It is precisely this competition for employees that does the most to increase salaries and wages for the residents of West Virginia. More directly, a high corporate income tax means that less money is available that could go toward paying workers higher wages or toward hiring additional employees. Also, since the money to pay the high tax must come from somewhere, it is likely that the price at which a business can sell its products or services while still making a profit will be higher than it otherwise would be, making the company less competitive with companies outside the state, and thus less likely to hold onto its market share.

Ironically, the main rationale for a high corporate net income tax in West Virginia has always been that West Virginia is a poor state with low wages. Because necessary tax revenues for the state must come from somewhere, the goal has been to spare "ordinary folks" as much as possible by passing on more of the state's tax burden to businesses instead of raising other taxes, such as property taxes on people's homes. While the goal of this policy is laudable, the policy itself is strongly self-defeating, virtually guaranteeing that a great many West Virginians will receive incomes that are substantially below average for the country as a whole. Our goal must be to improve incomes for West Virginians and keep property taxes on the low side.

Under the leadership of Governor Manchin, the corporate net income tax rate has been reduced to 8.5% at the present time, and is scheduled through a series of phased reductions to be reduced to 6.5% by 2014. *Unleashing Capitalism* recommends a much larger reduction. The Manchin administration has not championed this larger reduction because it does not see a way to make up for the "lost" revenue. If we look at the situation from the perspective of the Manchin administration, they may be correct. However, this is only because their perspective is much too limited. While it is certainly desirable to reduce the state corporate net income tax to the extent that Governor Manchin and the state legislature have achieved to date, genuine success for West Virginia requires a different approach: Not simply to make West Virginia *better* than it has been as regards its tax structure, but to make West Virginia *the best* among all the states as regards its tax structure.

There is a quantum difference between *better* and *best*.

Better may lead some businesses that are already on the fence to locate or expand in West Virginia. *Best* attracts attention from numerous businesses that otherwise would never have thought about locating in West Virginia. Publicizing *better* will cost the state a lot of money, while *best* is likely to generate a large quantity of free publicity because it will be seen as newsworthy by journalists everywhere. For a state that presently has a low ranking to become the best in the country (or even close to being the best) in one or more economic categories will draw a lot of favorable attention to West Virginia. It is an exciting and wholly realistic goal. The closer that West Virginia gets to reaching this goal, the more that its economic successes will expand its tax base, thus generating greater tax revenues than if tax rates had remained high.

Of course, becoming best, or close to the best, among all the states as regards its tax structure is not something that West Virginia can accomplish overnight, so we cannot ignore the possibility that tax revenues will temporarily be lost when major tax reductions are put into place. Governor Manchin and the state legislature have been on the right track in asking for phased rate reductions in order that revenues lost from a lessening tax rate be replaced by revenues from a broader tax base as business presence expands in West Virginia, and as business profits increase in absolute terms for new and existing businesses. But our state government should be much more ambitious as regards phased rate reductions that are further off in the future. More important, the overall rate of decrease should be speeded up substantially for the corporate net income tax and also for other business taxes: By 2014 (or 2015 at the latest), the rate for the corporate net income tax, for example, should be down to something like 4.5% rather than 6.5%. Rate reductions that are too far off into the future are not going to help businesses within the state that are struggling now, as many are, nor will it do enough now to attract new businesses.

In the meantime, West Virginia needs to publicize as widely as possible its goal of becoming the best state in the union as regards its business-friendly tax policies. It should publicize to the country at large and, indeed, to the world at large its intention to make good on the slogan: **Low Taxes, Least Red Tape, Highest Ethics.**

A big question: Will people believe us? Will people outside of West Virginia believe that our state is genuinely committed to making good on the above slogan?

There are a number of steps that West Virginians can take to ensure that the answer is *yes*:

* Support public officials who are committed to making West Virginia much more business-friendly.
* Publicize much more widely than at present all of West Virginia's natural advantages as described in Chapter 1.
* Remind the world at large that West Virginia is an especially cohesive state where people have what it takes to come together in order to serve a common purpose.
* Tell other West Virginians about the exciting possibilities for our state; insist that capitalism really can be defended in a way that appeals to virtually everyone regardless of their political orientation.

Because West Virginians have a strong sense of their own identity as West Virginians, if any state has a chance to make good on the slogan, **Low Taxes, Least Red Tape, Highest Ethics,** that state is West Virginia.

The more that West Virginia makes good on this slogan, the more prosperous it will become, and thus better able to make up for any temporary revenue losses.

The West Virginia Tax On Inventory, Machinery, And Equipment

This is a "personal property tax" that is applied to business. It directly taxes capital investment by a company, and as such is a burden to a company regardless of whether or not the company makes a profit in a given tax year. Thus, it increases the risk that is attached to business investment. This is true whether the investment is made by an expanding company within West Virginia or by an outside investor or company seeking to locate in West Virginia. Under the best of circumstances, business investments are risky. It is counterproductive for a state to increase that risk in such a direct fashion as does the current practice in West Virginia, when the state's number one business-oriented goal should be to encourage business investment. West Virginia's personal property tax on inventory, machinery, and equipment should be phased out. The goal should be to completely eliminate this tax within 5-8 years.

Critics will ask how West Virginia can make up for revenue that will be lost by the elimination of this tax. Some of these critics may be favorably disposed toward the position that was taken in recent years by the Manchin administration.

Governor Manchin did not advocate anything approaching the elimination of the state's personal property tax on inventory, machinery, and equipment. In a highly selective fashion, the Manchin administration and the state legislature reduced this tax as it applies, first, to corporate aircraft, such as company jets, and second as it applies to equipment and software purchased by high-technology businesses that are opening for the first time in West Virginia. However, few corporate planes were kept in West Virginia prior to July 1, 2009, when the tax reduction on aircraft took effect, and the high technology portion of the tax reduction applies only to new companies.

The selective nature of the recently enacted reductions is objectionable because it does not go anywhere nearly far enough. Someone might argue that it is at least a step in the right direction, but this is not a good argument because selective reductions in a tax that favor certain businesses or industries, or one or a few business practices but not others, are highly problematic for reasons that I discuss in a later section of this chapter.

The position taken here is that the West Virginia personal property tax on inventory, machinery, and equipment should be completely eliminated, following the recommendation in *Unleashing Capitalism*. But *Unleashing Capitalism* is wrong in recommending that lost revenue be recouped by having West Virginia impose a broad-based "value added tax" (VAT). As its name suggests, VAT is assessed on any increase in the value of goods that accrues to a company in the course of producing those goods. The increased value is the difference between what the company receives from the final sale of the goods and the amount it paid for materials and goods as inputs along the way in manufacturing goods as final products. While VAT is paid by the manufacturer, it inevitably gets passed on to the consumer.

Any type of VAT is a bad idea for West Virginia. At the time of this writing, only one other state, New Hampshire, has a VAT (except that they do not call it a VAT), which means that West Virginia would end up having an additional and unfamiliar type of tax, which would constitute a substantial disincentive for businesses to relocate in West Virginia from other states. Any new type of tax places a substantial burden on existing West Virginia businesses as well. Also, while the New Hampshire VAT is said to be a relatively simple tax (and the recommendation in *Unleashing Capitalism* is for a VAT that resembles the New Hampshire version), this is not true for any of the many European versions of VAT. They are typically assessed at several different stages in the manufacturing process; then amounts from earlier stages get subtracted from amounts at later stages in order that the manufacturer not end up paying twice for the same increase in value. All of this involves complex accounting procedures. Moreover, the entire VAT needs to be rebated if a product from Germany, for example, is sold in the U.S. in order for the German manufacturer not to be at a competitive disadvantage. Thus, if a West Virginia VAT was anything like the German VAT, there would need to be the same sort of rebate to allow goods from West Virginia to be competitive in other states and abroad.

West Virginia will not need a VAT if we dedicate ourselves with sufficient resolve to making **Low Taxes, Least Red Tape, Highest Ethics** a reality for West Virginia. Our state possesses all of the natural advantages for economic development that I mentioned in Chapter 1, and we have relatively low total state expenditures at the present time in absolute terms, primarily because West Virginia has been a poor state for so long. We have lots of room to grow economically. We have a state sales tax, as most states do, which we should keep in place with only a modest overall reduction at the present time. West Virginia should perhaps enact additional small specific reductions and adjustments to its sales tax as needed for the purpose of ensuring that West Virginia shoppers will not travel to adjacent states that have lower sales tax rates on specific items. Ideally, our sales tax rates will be low enough to encourage at least a small amount of shopper traffic in the opposite direction. The main point to keep in mind is that the West Virginia sales tax if kept near its present rate will provide much larger state revenues once the state experiences significant economic growth.

West Virginia also has a personal income tax, as do most other states, which we should keep in place but with modest, phased reductions over the next several years. This tax also will provide much larger state revenues once West Virginia experiences significant economic growth. I believe that substantial reductions in the West Virginia personal income tax will become possible at some time in the not-too-distant future.

The main obstacle to having West Virginia phase out its personal property tax on inventory, machinery, and equipment is that the West Virginia state constitution requires that education be funded from property taxes. One of the main advantages of living in West Virginia is that property taxes on one's home are significantly lower than in many other states—a near necessity in light of the lower wages and salaries in West Virginia. It is also a benefit that we will not want to lose when average wages and salaries increase substantially. West Virginians themselves ought to be allowed to hold onto most of those increases. The Manchin administration has supported amending the state constitution to allow counties to use other revenue sources for education. That is the right path to follow.

West Virginia's Business Franchise Tax

This is a tax that effectively is levied on the capital that a business has available to invest in order to grow or become more productive—the two outcomes that are most desirable as regards making our state more prosperous. It would be hard to imagine a tax that creates worse incentives than does the business franchise tax. A tax on profits kicks in only after profits are made, which is somewhat discouraging (so its rate should be kept low), but nowhere near as discouraging as a tax that is "upstream" from any profits that *may* (or may not) result from investment. The Manchin administration and the state legislature have reduced this tax, which will be wholly phased out of existence in 2015. Although sooner would be better, this is certainly the right direction in which to go.

Regarding all types of business-related taxes, including taxes on real estate and rights to resources, another point needs to be made. As everyone knows, starting, running, and expanding a business are risky under the best of circumstances. Part of the risk, obviously, lies in the possibility of misjudging how much money a company will earn on its operations. Another part lies in the possibility that assets owned by a business will lose a portion of their value at some time in the future; I am referring to assets that a company already owns or that it purchases in anticipation of expanding its operations, or that entrepreneurs purchase in anticipation of starting new businesses. Business-related assets include facilities, land, resources and rights to resources, and the company itself; taxes necessarily take away from the value of all such assets. When taxes on assets are high enough, ownership of the assets effectively ceases since the value of any use to which the assets might be put is equal to or less than the amount of the taxes. Reducing such taxes makes assets more valuable and business ventures less risky, and thus can serve as an additional strong incentive for business investment.

Selective Tax Incentives

The main reason for having selective tax incentives is to encourage new businesses to locate in West Virginia by giving them a break of some sort on their taxes. West Virginia presently makes extensive use of selective tax incentives, such as tax credits. They are bad for three main reasons. I have mentioned these reasons already in an earlier chapter.

First, tax credits are unfair. If a company is promised a break on its property taxes, for example, as a condition for moving to West Virginia, then this gives the new company an unfair advantage over companies already in the state with which the new company may compete. There will always be such companies already in the state. We should keep in mind that competition comes in many different forms. Thus, if someone in state government argues that offering tax credits will bring into West Virginia a wholly new type of company not presently located here, and that this new company will therefore not be competing with existing companies, we should reply that the new company will still compete for labor and resources and probably in several other ways as well even if it makes a new type of product or offers a new type of service. If, for example, an airline were to locate its corporate headquarters in West Virginia at a time when no other airline is headquartered here, there would still be competition because airlines compete with other forms of transportation, as well as competing for workers, resources, facilities, land, etc. And if a company pays lower taxes than another company but receives the same services, the shortfall must be made up somehow. Unfairness is inevitable.

The second reason why offering tax credits is bad is that tax credits violate basic capitalistic principles. When capitalism is functioning properly, companies will locate where conditions are most favorable in regard to all relevant economic factors. So we must ask: Why hasn't a particular company already decided to move to West Virginia? Why must this company be offered one or more tax credits as an inducement? There is only one possible answer: Because West Virginia is not, as things now stand, the best place for the company to locate. From the perspective of NDC, our number one response should be to take steps to fix things in order to ensure that West Virginia *will be the best place* for the company to locate. Offering tax credits papers over the problem, which is never a good thing to do. The problem will certainly apply to many other companies as well as the company that receives a particular tax credit. Offering tax credits obscures—or destroys outright—the information that would have been provided as regards West Virginia's desirability as a business location by the refusal of individual companies, or types of companies, to come here. This means that some of the important incentives for long-term business success disappear when tax credits are created.

Because tax credits represent political processes rather than market forces, their existence places obstacles in the path of business managers who are trying to make good business decisions for the future. It is difficult enough for even the most skillful and knowledgeable manager to make such decisions on the basis of an assessment of market realities (projections for sales, availability of resources, payroll costs, potential competition, and so on), simply because the business world is difficult and challenging. But it is true, at least, that market realities reflect factors that managers have been trained to recognize. Changes in these factors have types of causes that managers understand; it is their job to understand them. All of this is disrupted when tax credits are introduced, which means that an additional element of uncertainty is then present, namely political uncertainty, and this makes running a company more expensive and business investment more risky. Who can predict when new tax credits will be created that will change the competitive landscape for one's company?

The third reason why offering tax credits is bad for West Virginia is probably the most important: There are large costs in both the public and private sectors associated with tax credits, and these costs represent total losses in the overall scheme of things. Even considering costs borne only by West Virginia and its residents, it is hard to see how these costs can be outweighed by benefits. Consider first that, in the private sector, a company must spend a substantial amount of money in lobbying for a tax credit if it is to have a realistic opportunity of receiving one. Because tax credits by their very nature are selective, usually highly selective, the state cannot give them to all who might ask for them. Prospective companies must both compete with one another in seeking tax credits, and must curry favor with politicians. Money spent on lobbying efforts contributes nothing to a company's productivity. Likewise, as regards the public sector, legislators and the governor must devote a significant amount of time to dealing with lobbyists. This is time that does not go toward the making of better laws or greater executive effectiveness.

What is even worse is that, once it is in place as an acceptable policy, the practice of giving tax credits creates strong incentives for its expansion. A state legislator, for example, who is instrumental in "bringing a new company and new jobs" to his or her district via support for a tax credit will naturally emphasize this fact in a reelection bid, which will then invite opponents at election time to promise that they too will bring in new companies and new jobs. Each legislator and each candidate for office will try to raise the stakes as regards what is accomplished or what is promised. I have already mentioned in earlier chapters the incentives for corruption that are part and parcel with the entire political process that fosters tax credits.

As for the present situation in West Virginia, nothing is being done to reduce the extent to which the state grants tax credits or any other selective tax incentives, either by the legislature or by the governor. On the contrary, things have gotten worse. Because the recently enacted reductions in the West Virginia personal property tax on inventory, machinery, and equipment are highly selective, these reductions have created new tax credits, at the same time that no real steps are being taken to reduce the number of other types of tax credits or to curb the granting of tax credits in any of the various categories in which they are offered. The reason for all of this is easy to discover, as the following comparison will demonstrate. I offer the following analogy in the hope that readers will find it helpful.

I ask readers who are parents to think about the following important piece of advice on how to be a good parent: Never, ever give in to your young child when the child asks for something that you do not want the child to have. Suppose that you say no to a treat on a store shelf when you are shopping with your child, but the child throws a tantrum. The basic rule for good parenting is that you should never allow any exceptions to your policy of not giving in to your child's unreasonable demands. Otherwise, your child will know that you can be manipulated, even if this has happened only once. It will take a long time for you to drum this one occasion out of your child's mind. Likewise, if state government has allowed on only one or a few occasions for tax credits to be granted, this knowledge will be present in the minds of legislators and business promoters until such time as the state mandates that it will henceforth grant no tax credits at all. Until that happens, the temptation will exist for legislators to gain an elective edge, or business people to gain a competitive edge, by pursuing tax credits—by reviving a dormant policy, creating new categories of tax credits, or making a special plea for a tax credit to be granted in a purportedly unique set of circumstances.

The position taken in this book is that West Virginia should legislate immediately that no new tax credits will be granted under any circumstances, and that existing tax credits will be phased out insofar as this can be done without breaking promises that state government has already made to existing businesses.

Genuine Transparency—
A Promising New Idea To Help Control Spending

One of the most important ways to reduce taxes is to reduce state spending. If West Virginia could reduce the amount of money that it spends by eliminating or scaling back on outdated or inefficient programs and policies, it could scale back substantially on taxes, other things being equal. Control of state spending absolutely must go hand-in-hand with reductions in taxes. How can this be accomplished? There are many answers, quite a few of them addressed elsewhere in this book. I mention here a relatively new idea for putting pressure on government to spend its money wisely: Increase to the maximum the extent to which a state makes available online detailed information about its budget and the processes that are involved in the creation of its budget. While every state at the present time posts some of this information online, some states do a much better job than others.

At the time of this writing, the state of Florida has recently put into place a web-based mechanism for governmental budgetary transparency (at transparencyflorida.gov) that promises to be among the best. Posted information is to be updated nightly, and will eventually include most aspects of the state's budget, along with accounts of the legislative and deliberative processes that yielded all of the different budget figures in all of the different categories. The creation of this website would seem, at this early stage, to be a large step in the right direction since it provides a thoroughgoing counter force to the incentives that legislators, bureaucrats, and government executives usually face. These incentives count toward budgetary secrecy: It is usually in the interest of someone running for reelection to keep secret all budgetary information except what will be seen as favorable by supporters at the ballot box. But if voters can readily view up-to-date information about the entirety of a state's budget, it will be much harder for officials to craft a budget that favors one group of voters—who are told in a loud voice about the benefits to them—while not helping, or even harming, another group of voters who are told nothing. Voters can play a much more prominent role in helping to keep the budgets of their states under control at election times. Transparency allows voters and citizens to bring pressure to bear on how legislators vote on bills during legislative sessions. The same pressure can be brought to bear on all of the important decisions that a governor makes in putting a budget together, and on other legislation proposed by a governor. This is especially important in a state like West Virginia where the governor plays a larger role in creating a budget than do the governors in some other states.

Everything that I have just said about transparency at the state level applies at the federal level as well. Since a substantial portion of state expenses are mandated by the federal government, transparency at the federal level can translate into pressure being applied by the citizens and the governments of all the states to reduce federal mandates for state spending. Federal mandates constitute a substantial portion of all state budgets. If voters had ready access online to all aspects of the federal budget, and not just the parts of it that may appear favorable to particular groups of voters (as disclosed to them by candidates for office and media people covering campaigns), these voters would be in a much better position to help restrain federal spending, along with mandates for spending at the state level. Candidates for the Senate, the House, and the Presidency would need to pay close attention to all of this new information available to voters.

Chapter 12.
Least Red Tape, West Virginia

It is human nature to want to improve things—for oneself, one's family, one's community, one's state, one's country, or the world at large. In the private sector, everything a person does for the sake of achieving some type of improvement is subject to continuous competition from the efforts of other people who are themselves attempting to bring about improvements through *their own* efforts. This is true whether we are talking about a better salary for oneself, running a better business that serves both oneself and others, coming up with a new idea or invention that may serve a great many people, or undertaking a new charitable endeavor to help people in need. In virtually every situation, we must prove ourselves against the competition—the other people who want to receive higher salaries for themselves, start their own new businesses, operate their own charities, and so on. Nothing worthwhile is ever easy, apart from the circumstances of a few rare individuals who seem to be just plain lucky!

The other side of the coin is that continuous competition provides checks and balances that are extremely important to ensure that, for the most part anyway, one person's salary is not way out of line with other people's salaries, that individual businesses remain assets to their communities, and that charities remain cost-effective and worthwhile.

In the public sector, the situation is very different. There is always initial competition for a new law or program because other legislators, citizens, and interested parties are all trying hard to get their own bills passed, or their own pet projects supported, or their own spheres of government expanded to serve what is judged by them to be worthy purposes. However, once a new law is passed or a new government entity is created, competition dwindles dramatically because no mechanism is any longer in place that is designed expressly to ensure that checks and balances continue to function. As a consequence, while private sector competition continues indefinitely to drive inefficient businesses and business practices out of existence, in the sphere of government almost everything tends to get locked in and barnacle-encrusted. Most government creations tend to become more complex and burdensome as time goes by.

Citizens pay an increasingly high price for this, especially if they are trying to run their own companies. Someone who wishes to create or expand a business faces not just the expected ongoing competition from other individuals who wish to create or expand their own businesses, but an ever larger tangle of laws and regulations. If West Virginia is to become the best state in the union, which it absolutely can and should become, it must meet this challenge head-on so as to achieve for itself a clear competitive advantage over other states. It must ensure that **Least Red Tape, West Virginia** becomes a reality. It must take large, bold steps in the direction of making all facets of state government user-friendly.

A window of opportunity is now open for our state to become the first state in the country whose citizens understand exactly what must be done in order to reinstate checks and balances into the laws, regulations, programs, bureaus, and bureaucracies of our state government. Toward this end, no one needs to reinvent the wheel. It has long been known that effective steps can be taken to create the sorts of checks and balances to which I am referring in order to guarantee that government is not a burden. What has usually been absent is the *public will* to take those steps. The reason why the public will has largely been absent is that too few voters have understood the underlying issues. Or if they have understood the issues, they have not acted on their knowledge at the ballot box, and they have not done enough to pass on their understanding to other voters. West Virginia's voters now possess a golden opportunity to become an emulated exception. We are a small state, we share a stronger sense of common purpose than do the citizens of most other states, each of us can get out the word to our friends and neighbors, and we can prove to all non-West Virginians that good things happen when enough voters understand basic economic ideas and how to implement those ideas.

Sunset Provisions

This is the most important idea. To attach a sunset provision to a new law, regulation, or governmental entity is to place a time limit on the law, regulation, or governmental entity, such as five years on a new regulation for businesses. At the end of five years from when the regulation takes effect, the regulation must be reviewed by the body responsible for creating it, such as the state legislature or the appointed members of a state agency, or else by a commission expressly created to enforce sunset provisions. Cost-benefit analysis must be applied to de-

173

termine whether or not the law should remain in effect. Complete transparency must be maintained as regards the evaluative processes to ensure that citizens have an opportunity to learn about the bases on which government officials decide to keep, alter, or abolish existing laws, regulations, or governmental entities.

The main rationale behind the idea of sunset provisions is to recreate something like the competitive pressures that were in effect when a law was originally passed, or agency rules and policies were originally being debated. At that earlier time, as regards the example of legislation, there was competition from legislators who favored different laws or no law. The various possibilities were examined, compared, and debated. Our goal as reformers should be to recreate on a regular, continuing basis the essential aspects of this original competition in order to ensure that government does not continue to grow unchecked, and that any new law has lived up to the original expectations and continues to yield substantially more good than harm. Our goal should be to ensure that life in West Virginia does not become subject to an increasingly greater complexity of restrictions that hamper business growth and hold back the economy of our state.

You may be asking yourself: If sunset provisions are such a good thing, why don't we—as voters—hear more about them? Why doesn't West Virginia already have an extensive, tried and true sunset program in place? There are two main reasons.

Voter knowledge. The first reason is that for good things to happen in the political sphere, there is no substitute for voter knowledge. But voters in West Virginia and elsewhere do not know a lot about the sunset idea, for one reason because it is not an especially glamorous idea. There have not existed sufficient incentives on the part of people in government or the media to promote it. When legislators and governors report to their constituents, they are, they believe, more likely to appear to be serving their constituents' interests if they (the legislators or governors) can report "positive" accomplishments—new laws, new programs, new governmental entities, etc.—that promise new benefits. It would not be as glamorous to report that the only accomplishments this year were, first, scaling back or abolishing some existing laws or programs and second, keeping some other programs exactly as they had been, after spending a significant amount of time evaluating them.

Let it be said that West Virginia is an exception: Voters here *do* judge that modifying and abolishing existing governmental creations is glamorous. Voters here *do* judge that spending time examining governmental creations, and then deciding in some cases that nothing should be done is glamorous. West Virginians *do* get excited about these processes because we understand how important it is to keep government from becoming stagnant and bloated.

West Virginia voters will become even more excited by the increases in state prosperity that result when word gets out that West Virginia is unique in being a state where, first, appropriate sunset provisions are in place, and second, where voters in the state understand the great value of sunset provisions, so that people who locate their businesses here can expect that our state's commitment to the existence of sunset laws will continue. Voter understanding and support for something are the best guarantee that it will be around for a long time, as I have said. People everywhere will notice what is happening here, especially if we make a strong early showing, which will virtually guarantee that we will receive a lot of free publicity for our efforts.

Choosing the right areas. The second reason why West Vir-

175

ginia does not already have an extensive, well-oiled sunset program in place is that sunset provisions need to be restricted to the right sorts of laws, regulations, programs, and government entities. We do not want sunset provisions in the wrong areas. But distinguishing between the right and wrong areas can be tricky. Of course, we do not want sunset provisions to apply to constitutional protections, case law that has built up around those protections, or to any enactments of government that are so important that we *do* want to think of them as being engraved in stone once we have won the battle to get them enacted. And it is natural for all legislators when contemplating their own pet projects, along with other fervent supporters of those projects, to suppose that their particular projects ought to be exceptions to the sunset idea.

I suggest the following practical approach as a step in the right direction. Let us agree to the existence of a presumption in favor of individual freedom and against placing restrictions on individual freedom. Accordingly, let us support the enactment of a general sunset statute for West Virginia which stipulates that every new law or regulation that *restricts* freedom—which tells people that they cannot do something that before the passage of the law they could do—be subject to a sunset provision. New laws or regulations that do not restrict freedom—which do not tell people that they cannot do something that before the passage of the law they could do, or which decree that people can now do something that before the passage of the law they could not do—will not automatically be subject to a sunset provision but will need to be debated case by case in order to determine whether or not a sunset provision is called for.

I turn next to another important proposal for ensuring that **Least Red Tape, West Virginia** will become a reality.

A Commission For "Simplifying West Virginia"

The governor of West Virginia should create a blue-ribbon commission whose charge is to study all state programs and policies with the aim of finding simpler ways to accomplish the very same essential goals. I do not mean to imply that none of the goals of existing programs and policies need to be changed, of course, but only to propose a proper division of labor. Other arms of government can, and should, examine the worthiness of the goals of various programs and policies. We need a separate effort devoted exclusively to simplification. Candidates for possible simplification include all of the steps that must be taken when someone applies for a permit or license to do just anything for which a permit or license is required; the paperwork (or online steps) required for the calculation and payment of any and all taxes, and any and all fees for the renewal of licenses and permits; the reporting requirements for compliance with laws and regulations pertaining to all types of businesses and nonprofit organizations, including environmental, safety, and social justice-oriented laws and regulations. Overall, the "Simplifying West Virginia Commission" would make recommendations to the Governor for simplifying executive orders and directives; to heads of state agencies for simplifying requirements of all types; and to the state legislature to pass simpler laws that accomplish the same essential goals as present laws (unless the goals themselves also need to be changed).

I recognize that some people within state government are already concerned with simplifying existing laws and procedures. The general idea that I am proposing is not exactly new. Again, there is no need to reinvent the wheel. Having a blue-ribbon commission in place will, however, draw attention to the worthy endeavors of people already committed to the task of simplification, while greatly expanding their endeavors, and also send a strong message to voters and everyone else that West Virginians understand how important simplification in government is.

The number one benefit from achieving greater simplification in government is a reduction in compliance costs for businesses. We want every West Virginia business to devote as little time and money as possible to adhering to the letter of the law in our state. Of course, we must have regulations, taxes, and restrictions on what people can do, and all such measures are inherently onerous. Let us, therefore, go all out to ensure that these measures are as close as possible to being painless.

After all, if nearly painless dentistry is possible (we see advertisements for it these days), why can we not move much closer to having painless government?

Many people in West Virginia and elsewhere who might otherwise consider creating their own companies are frightened off by the complexity of the start-up process. Yet, innovation in business is required now more than ever before. A single individual with a new idea can build a company that challenges the world's best multinational corporations if that person is given half a chance. The odds for success are greatest if the person is genuinely encouraged by a state that is openly grateful for the creation of new jobs and new businesses, and expresses that gratitude by (among other steps) taking seriously state-wide efforts to simplify all of the stages in the business startup process, and also doing the exact same thing for all of the steps involved in running a business after it has been established.

The second benefit from achieving greater simplification is less direct but still very important: We want government to be easier to understand by people both in the business world and outside of the business world. Whatever is inherently simpler is easier to understand, and whatever is easier to understand is likely to attract more of the good kinds of attention. Our state will become a much better place if large numbers of citizens take a lot more interest in the nuts and bolts of government regulations and programs. More good ideas for improving how government operates will result. More people will speak out against bad regulations and policies. Transparency in state government that is powered by the type of online postings that are described in the previous chapter will become accessible to a lot more people.

Chapter 13.
Highest Ethics, West Virginia

At a time when it is increasingly true that goods, capital, and workers can move easily from state to state, and when people can shop almost anywhere electronically, if not in person, a state must have a lot to offer if it is to be successful in competition against other states. It must possess a sound political, legal, and economic system in order to protect basic rights and to be able to offer attractive economic opportunities. It must provide people with a secure place to live, and it must safeguard private property and the accumulation of assets. It must safeguard the environment. It must keep taxes and compliance costs at low levels. It must control crime effectively, both through the successful prosecution of criminals and through the reduction of major causes of crime. And it must possess moral attitudes on the part of its citizens toward their fellow human beings. In other words, a successful state is one where everyone is treated well—owners of businesses, employees, entrepreneurs, consumers, homemakers, those who teach the young, and those who care for the old.

The possession of moral attitudes should embrace all West

Virginians—voters, elected officials, government employees, the members of all professions and trades, investors, and so on. For **Highest Ethics, West Virginia** to contribute to making our state number one in the country, moral attitudes must be on display in all of our state's institutions and ways of conducting its affairs. Changes are needed if this to become true. Fortunately, bringing the required changes into existence is easier now than it would have been at any time in the past.

Over the long course of history, improvements in governments and social conditions have usually been slow in coming because the efforts of reformers have been pitted against the enormous power of entrenched leaders, vested interests, and the perception that established ways of doing things should not be changed because Awe have always done things that way." What was needed in order to speed up the processes of reform—something that did not fully exist until now—was strong external pressure upon governments and societies to improve. That pressure now exists in the form of active and strong competition among states and countries. However, for the pressure to be translated into genuine reform in the domain of ethics, it must be fully recognized. Voters need to see that one of the best ways for West Virginia to compete successfully against other states is for West Virginia to be a place where everyone is treated well, and where people both within the state and outside of the state *perceive* that everyone is treated well in West Virginia. West Virginians have always been friendly and helpful people. No one can ask for better neighbors. Let us see to it that this naturally beneficent and fairminded attitude on our part is extended to all of our institutions and ways of doing business.

The West Virginia Ethics Commission, established in 1989 under Governor Gaston Caperton, is a step in the right direction. It focuses on preventing unethical conduct by elected officials and public employees in situations where conflicts of interest exist. It provides excellent guidelines and effective grievance procedures. Our state benefits a lot from having the WV Ethics Commission, but more attention to ethical issues is needed.

West Virginia's Legal System

A good place to begin is by taking a look at the West Virginia Supreme Court, the members of which are elected while standing for election as members of a political party. What we have is a highly partisan process that hurts West Virginia in competition with other states to attract new businesses and business investments. The people of West Virginia need to recognize that this is so. *Unleashing Capitalism*, referred to in an earlier chapter, documents the extent to which the quality of a state's legal system suffers when a state's supreme court justices are elected in a partisan manner as in West Virginia. By comparison to other ways to select justices, it is fair to say that legal system quality suffers the most under the type of system in place in West Virginia, which exists in only seven other states at the present time. Candidates for the Court are subject to the most corrupting sorts of political pressures. By contrast, states where justices are elected, but where candidates run on name only with no party affiliation, experience somewhat better legal system quality, while states where justices are not elected at all, but appointed instead, experience the highest legal system quality.

Governor Manchin championed an effort to have candidates for the West Virginia Supreme Court receive funds from the state to run their campaigns, thus reducing the corruptive effect of having partisan candidates rely entirely on campaign donations. However, research indicates that, while this would be an improvement, it is not the best solution, and that what West Virginia should do instead is move to a system where justices are appointed. One of the main arguments against appointing justices has always been that corruptive influences are present here as well since an aspiring justice needs to please the governor (who of course belongs to a political party) or whoever else has the authority to appoint justices. While this argument does have some force, corruptive influences present when justices are appointed are likely to be less pronounced than when justices are elected.

The key to ensuring that a system of appointive justices is fair lies in electing the right sorts of people to public office, because among them will be the individuals who end up appointing justices, or having an influence on those who make the appointments. I am referring to candidates for public office who express a strong commitment to moral values in their campaigns, and whose resumes suggest that they will live up to their campaign promises.

The other important step is for West Virginia to adopt the online transparency mechanism described in Chapter 11. Voters will then be able to scrutinize the actions of elected officials much more easily and closely in order to determine whether an official genuinely possesses a commitment to moral principles or instead makes decisions or casts votes primarily on the basis of political expediency or personal aggrandizement. Elected officials who know that their actions are being scrutinized closely will, naturally, behave better. Some potential candidates with dubious resumes may choose not to run for public office in the first place. Other candidates will resolve from the beginning to behave in a thoroughly responsible way. With a political climate in West Virginia that is much more demanding morally, we can expect that high quality appointments will be made to the West Virginia Supreme Court, once an appointive system is adopted.

In the next section, I say more about how our state should go about creating a morally more demanding political climate.

Morality In Public Life

The place to start, as with the economic dimension of government, is with higher levels of voter awareness and commitment. A great many people have their hearts in the right place, morally speaking, regardless of the state or country in which they live. They want to do the right thing, and they want to support candidates for public office who are strongly committed to moral values. This is unquestionably true in a state like West Virginia. But morality is a difficult concept. I know this all too well from my many years of teaching ethics courses to a wide diversity of students at West Virginia University. I know that many individuals who have their hearts in the right place may disagree among themselves when it comes to focusing on specific moral principles and values.

I believe that Universal Moral Pluralism as described in Chapter 8 is sufficiently broad and flexible in scope that people with diverse backgrounds can find in it a basis for agreement when questions are raised about the moral standing of candidates for public office:

> * Do these candidates believe strongly in upholding and protecting everyone's basic rights? Do they understand that doing this is the number one job of government?
> * Do they believe that moral people, and good governments as well, recognize an obligation to help people in need who cannot adequately help themselves?

* Do they believe that all of us, whether we are in the private sector or in government, should do our part to help make the world a better place, and especially to make our own country and our own state better places, but that we also have a quite separate obligation to look after ourselves?

* Do the *lives* of candidates for public office, insofar as we have knowledge about them, seem to be consistent with the sorts of moral commitments that I have just described, and which the candidates themselves should be willing to articulate if they are asked about such matters?

* Do the lives and beliefs of these individuals seem to be consistent with a recognition that every human life has intrinsic value (which means from a religious perspective that everyone is "precious in the eyes of God")?

As I remarked earlier, what I say about Universal Moral Pluralism in this book is not meant to be the last word, but rather is intended as a point of focus when people come together in making moral judgments and assessments, such as when voters and citizens are evaluating people in business or government, or people running for public office. I will be the first to acknowledge that my version of Universal Moral Pluralism is probably not exactly what readers think of first when they think about basic moral values. But I feel confident that most people have something like my Universal Moral Pluralism in the back of their mind when they think about answering important moral questions. I find a lot of support for Universal Moral Pluralism, or something very much like it, when I talk to my students, for example. An earlier version of Universal Moral Pluralism is featured in *A Good Day's Work: Sus-*

taining Ethical Behavior and Business Success, mentioned above, of which I am co-author. This book has been very favorably received. I am confident that any initially skeptical readers, once they spend time thinking about the relevant issues, will come around to seeing that my list of basic values has a lot to recommend it:

* Working to improve society as a whole, or a substantial portion of society
* Fulfilling oneself
* Helping people in need
* Protecting the basic rights of every individual.

Readers will see that this list draws upon the moral intuitions of a great many people. They will see that this list of values is needed in its entirety in order to capture all that is included in the recognition that the lives of all human beings have intrinsic value.

To return to the question of how best to implement **Highest Ethics, West Virginia:** What I would like to see is a situation where voters at election times scrutinize the moral commitments of candidates, and then continue to do the same thing once an individual is elected to office. Let us hold to the fire the feet of everyone in government! Let it become known that voters in West Virginia cannot be bamboozled by their elected officials or governmental appointees. Let it be known that we expect our leaders in government to be genuine public servants, and that we never look favorably upon individuals who game the system for their own advantage.

Doing what I am suggesting here is made easier when we have some general moral guidelines in front of us (such as the principles of Universal Moral Pluralism); when other people are on the same page that we are on, morally speaking, and are talking about it (and writing letters to the editor, emailing their friends, and posting observations to our state's leading political blogs and to social media); and when we have in front of us some specific guidelines, such as those in this book, for how moral values and principles should be applied in government and business. In addition, there are steps that we all can take toward strengthening our own moral integrity and the moral integrity of others. I discuss some of these steps in the next section.

Moral Integrity

When I read news stories about public figures who have fallen from grace because of moral lapses, I often feel very sorry for these people, many of whom have a lot to be proud of in their careers apart from the acts that disgraced them. These people's own inner incentives let them down. In fact, many basically good people end up ruining their careers or their lives because their moral outlook is not deeply enough ingrained in their character. Such individuals are not properly armed against the temptation "just this once" to do something that is not entirely ethical. They pay a high price when they are found out. We do a huge favor to these people—who could be ourselves or someone close to us—when we help them to become more firmly committed to a moral outlook on life. How should we go about doing this?

A comparison to physical exercise is helpful, I believe.

We all know that there are two ways to exercise, an easy way and a hard way. The easy way, unfortunately, is possible only when we are already in good physical shape, and our bodies themselves just naturally "want" to exercise. We then feel good when exerting ourselves, except perhaps when we push ourselves unusually hard. The second way to exercise, the hard way, is what invariably faces us when we are out of shape physically. Then we do not feel good when exercising, especially at first. Our bodies do not want to exercise, but we know that we should exercise if our health permits it. Moral behavior is something like this.

There is an easy way and a hard way to behave morally. In both types of situation, hopefully, it will be true that we fundamentally want to do the morally right thing, but in the one type of situation doing what is morally right comes naturally to us, so it is easy, or at least relatively easy. In the other type of situation, doing what is morally right may involve a struggle: We do want to do the right thing, at least in a *general* way, but as far as specific behaviors are concerned, we are rusty, or it may be that for some situations we have never even begun to figure out exactly what the right thing to do is. We have not become habituated to doing the right thing.

Part of the problem is that we may find ourselves in possession of inclinations not to do the right thing, and we must then fight against those inclinations—just as a person who goes jogging after having not exercised in a long time must fight against the inclination to stop immediately and rest. In a fight against an inclination to compromise their values, people sometimes win the fight, and sometimes lose the fight. Sometimes people do not even attempt to fight against their nonmoral inclinations. One way to think about moral integrity is to say that we want to "fix the fight"—take steps to ensure that moral behavior wins out in all of the conflicts between moral and less-than-moral inclinations.

What makes the most difference as to how much success will be achieved when efforts are made to strengthen moral integrity? Where other people are concerned—whose moral behavior and decision-making we would like to influence—what usually works best is positive reinforcement for a "job well done." A job is well done in the fullest sense when a person has acted both effectively and morally. The main goal of positive reinforcement in relation to strengthening moral integrity is to get people to repeat morally exemplary behavior in order to strengthen it—just as repetition of physical activity strengthens muscles. We want completely moral behavior on the part of individuals in both government and business to become a strongly ingrained habit. Therefore, we should do everything we can to induce people to repeat any good behavior that they display. We should support them (with our votes, money, patronage as consumers, kind words, or help of any other kind) when good behavior occurs, and we should withhold support when it does not occur. Above all, we must never, ever enable elected officials to continue to behave immorally by reelecting them. We may be tempted to do this if an elected official is helping us, or our own special interests, or the district in which we live, but at the expense of behaving ethically in a broader sense. An example is an official who "brings home the bacon" via legislative earmarks that are unfair or wasteful, as many earmarks are. We must never give in to the temptation to reelect such a person. Our goal should be to support only morally exemplary behavior so as to reinforce it.

Likewise, when we are trying to strengthen our own moral integrity, what we are aiming for is repetition of our own praiseworthy moral decision-making, and a lessening of those times when our decision-making is anything less than praiseworthy. To be successful, we must consciously and deliberately focus on our own behavior and make an effort to control it when this is needed. With practice and effort, we can strengthen our control of our own behavior, which is to say that we can strengthen our will power and self-control. Doing so will pay off in many areas of our lives. Of course, before we can repeat moral behavior

190

and effective moral decision-making, we must know exactly what we ought to be doing. This requires both moral understanding and the mastery of what I like to refer to as "moral skills." Sometimes we need to learn new moral skills.

A person who has moral skills knows the best things to say and to do in all of the different kinds of circumstances that call for making moral decisions and acting on those decisions. A person who does not know the best things to do or say will probably not act in the best ways or say the best things, and therefore will not reinforce in himself/herself, or in others, the best responses. There are important moral skills for every area of life—business, politics, friendship, marriage, parenting, the professions, investing, sports, and so on. The general topic of moral skills covers a lot of territory, and goes beyond the scope of this book. My purpose in mentioning it here is simply to get readers to focus more sharply on the right sorts of questions to ask of themselves and others in regard to strengthening moral integrity.

* Do I know what the right course of action is in a given situation? (Have I spent time thinking about the moral values that apply to the situation, and about how people whom I admire might respond?)
* Am I reinforcing the right sorts of behaviors in myself and others?
* Am I making it easier in my own case to "just naturally" do what is right?
* Am I being careful not to do anything that will reinforce someone else's behaviors and habits that are less than ideal? (For example, am I being sure that I do not enable elected officials to build their careers around pleasing special interests at the expense of larger moral goals?)

* Am I being careful not to reinforce actions and habits in my business associates and friends that fall short of what I know to be morally the best?

One Last Word

Because managers, in both business and government, typically have more influence on the behavior of other people than non-managers, I will end this Chapter by reminding readers that points made in Chapter 9 are important for implementing **Highest Ethics, West Virginia.**

Managers are to be found in both the public and private sectors. One of our goal as West Virginians should be moral improvement all across the state in the area of management, both in business and in government. In Chapter 9, I suggested that the Quality and Ethics Management (QEM) movement provides the best guidelines for making management more moral.

Let it be said that West Virginia is a state whose citizens are aware of the principles of good management. For those of us who are managers ourselves, let us manage well. For those of us who serve under managers, let us appreciate good management when it occurs, and tell our managers that we appreciate it. Let us also speak up, if we can, when our managers are not doing a good job in treating us respectfully and helping us to perform at our best.

Chapter 14.
Voters as CEOs

How do we get the people who serve in government to respond consistently to the right sorts of incentives? What we want, but often do not have, is for people in government to work toward the betterment of society as a whole and for the long term, instead of responding to incentives provided by special interests and short-term interests.

The Textile Industry And President Reagan

Consider the example of the textile industry that is discussed in Chapter 6. The U.S. has attempted to protect the domestic textile industry with tariffs that go back to the early nineteenth century, including large tariffs imposed in 1816 and 1828, high tariffs during the 1930s, and tariffs that were increased under Presidents Kennedy and Nixon. The real shocker is that tariffs on textiles were increased even under President Reagan. During his years in office, Reagan supported major tax reductions and successful efforts by the Federal Reserve to stabilize the currency, which together helped to strengthen the American economy. Reagan is rightly praised for his understanding of the requirements for a strong economy. Why, then, did he allow tariffs on textiles to increase during his presidency? Was the textile industry a special case, exempt from the general rule that increasing tariffs is economically hurtful? (Exceptions do exist, such as when a temporary tariff increase is part of a longer-term negotiating strategy to reduce tariffs both at home and abroad.)

It was not a special case. In fact, the American textile industry was not helped over the long term by the Reagan-era tariffs or by any other tariffs. I noted in Chapter 6 that the National Cotton Council of America correctly described U.S. textiles in 2006 as an "industry in crisis." The explanation for Reagan's behavior is that he bowed to pressure from those whom he judged to be important political supporters. Presidents have always done this, regardless of their personal beliefs, moral commitments, or party affiliation. Reagan was firmly committed to supporting capitalism, and he did support capitalism after a fashion (and more strongly than many of his predecessors or successors), but he also supported, or at least permitted, numerous anti-capitalist measures, including federal deficits that were huge by the standards of the time.

Clearly, if capitalism is to be supported successfully, we must get away from the "politics as usual" mentality that is prevalent in the United States and most other democratic countries. What I have in mind requires a rethinking of the way that democratic governments should function.

What Is The Proper Way For Democracy To Function?

Most people would give the following answer: The job of voters is to inform themselves about the candidates who are running for office, then pick the candidates who seem to have the best views and strongest personal qualifications. The job of the individuals who end up being elected is to run the country, or the state or the city. If the voters are well-informed or lucky, they will have chosen individuals who told the truth about their views and qualifications when campaigning, who do their best to keep their pre-election promises after being elected, and who turn out to be thoroughly competent in carrying through on what they said they would do.

What I have just described is the view of democratic government that most people accept. It entails a clear separation of roles: Voters select the officials, then the officials run the country or the state. Once elected, the officials are in charge. They are effectively the CEOs.

The problem with this view of how democratic government functions is that, as I have been saying throughout this book, elected officials are subject to strong incentives that count against having the officials do an all-around good job:

* Incentives to hide the truth about capitalism
* Incentives to hide the real consequences of many specific pieces of legislation
* Incentives to never mention "what might have been" if government programs had not siphoned off money from the private sector
* Incentives to tolerate or encourage cozy relationships between government regulators and the companies and industries being regulated
* Incentives to sometimes flat-out lie to voters

It is true also that elected officials who do a good job can point to their record of genuine accomplishments at reelection time, and this fact is a motivator for elected officials actually to do a good job. But important though it is, the incentive to do a good job is all too easily weakened in today's world by several different factors: frequent disagreements among voters as to what actually counts as a good job on the part of elected officials; the fact that people in government frequently do not know what actually constitutes doing a good job because they have been so busy learning how to be successful politicians that they have not had time to learn much about economics or other relevant disciplines; the ease with which people in government may appear to have done a good job when in reality they have acted primarily to please their constituents. As regards the last of these points, what usually happens is that elected official talk only about the specific benefits that they have fostered for a select group of their constituents while ignoring the accompanying harms or indifference to the interests of other people. This is what usually constitutes their "record of genuine accomplishments."

There are also *internal* incentives that are distinct from the external incentives that I have just discussed. These internal incentives include moral beliefs that motivate elected officials to work toward making society a better place, and not to give in to temptations for the sake of being elected or reelected. The obvious problem here is that moral incentives often count against someone's being elected since the person may end up not making the sorts of deals with voting blocks that opponents are willing to make and that help the opponents to win. In short, the democratic process itself tends all too often to select against individuals with strong moral beliefs.

Is there a solution? I believe that there is, but first I need to say more about the notion that elected officials are the people who ought to be in charge.

More About Elected Officials As Ceos

I ask readers, first, to contrast "elected officials as CEOs" with actual CEOs in the business world. It is true that CEOs in business face incentives to put their own careers first at the expense of doing their best to make their companies successful, and some CEOs in business yield to these incentives, occasionally in a big way (Enron comes to mind). But most business CEOs also face strong pressures every day to make their companies profitable, and profitability is hard to fake. Enron and Bernard L. Madoff Investment Securities are examples of companies where CEOs did for a long time get away with faking success, but such companies are rare. To a large extent, CEOs in business realize that the best way to achieve success and happiness for themselves is to help make their companies genuinely successful, both at the present time and into the future.

The world of politics is very different from the world of business:

* Elected officials have *much more leeway* than CEOs in business to hide the truth about how well or poorly they are doing their jobs.
* Elected officials may not even bother to learn the truth about how well they are doing their jobs.
* Elected officials can use their time in office as a springboard to other elective offices or private sector jobs, while leaving behind a legacy of poor performance that others must deal with.
* All too often, elected officials are able to get away with placing blame on others—the opposing political party, the media, Big Business, Wall Street, the global economy, etc. Business CEOs cannot so easily blame their own mistakes on others.

Unquestionably, there are serious problems with the "elected officials as CEOs" view of democratic government.

Voters As Ceos

I recommend that we adopt a new view of how democratic government should function: I call it the "voters as CEOs" view of democratic government. The idea is that voters should adopt the mind set of a CEO. This means, first, thinking in terms of the big picture—how well the country or state is doing now and into the future. Second, it means that, as much as they can, voters should look over the shoulders of all their elected officials, and let those officials know that they are being watched, and that they (the voters) are paying the same sort of close attention to how well the country or the state is being run that CEOs pay to how well their companies are being run. Voters should remind themselves frequently that elected officials are likely to be motivated by the wrong sorts of incentives, and therefore must be kept in line by the voters, who are motivated by the *right sorts of incentives,* at least to a much larger extent than is the case for elected officials.

After all, voters want things to go well in all areas of their lives, for themselves, their children if they have children, their friends, and their fellow citizens. Voters do have strictly partisan interests also, needless to say. But if voters focus mainly on their partisan interests, they will continue to enable elected officials to proceed with "politics as usual." None of us wants that, once we think about it.

The "voters as CEOs" mind set applies especially well at the level of state government because of the relatively narrow scope of state government. This is not to say that it does not apply at the federal level as well, but I will focus here on the state level.

The Ceo Mind Set For West Virginia Voters

In West Virginia, the first thing for "voters as CEOs" to do is familiarize themselves with all of the statistics that show how well or poorly our state is doing in comparison to other states. A good place to start is with information provided by the Bureau of Economic Analysis, which provides rankings of states' per capita income, among other measures. As of 2009, for example, as I mentioned earlier, West Virginia was ranked 47th, an improvement over 2008, when West Virginia was ranked 49th! The Corporation for Enterprise Development provides comparative rankings of the states in several different categories. For 2010, it assigns a grade of F for the quality of health care in West Virginia. It reports that eighth grade students do poorly in comparison to other states in tests of math, science, reading, and writing. It reports also that a college education in West Virginia has become less affordable than in recent past years.

On the positive side, Moody's Investors Service has assigned an Aa1 rating to a recent bond issue in West Virginia, namely the state's $35 million General Obligation State Road Refunding Bonds Series 2010A. This is a high rating, and is better than ratings for West Virginia's bonds in the recent past. It is a reflection of the fact that West Virginia has done a good job in recent years in managing its money. As a poor state, West Virginia does not have a lot of money to manage by comparison to most other states, but it has done a reasonably good job with the money that it has.

Where do voters as CEOs fit in? Well, just as CEOs in business absolutely must know how well their companies are doing in comparison to competing companies in order to keep their own companies competitive and profitable, voters as CEOs need to know how well their state is doing in comparison to other states, if they are to support measures that allow their state to be successful. Voters as CEOs need to know what

199

is really going on, not just what elected officials may say is going on.

For the typical business CEO, extensive comparative information is always on the CEO's desk or computer screen. Then, when a company's performance begins to slip, the first thing that a CEO must do is convey a detailed picture of what is happening to heads of divisions and departments, sales staff, designers, marketers, and so on. By contrast, governors and legislators over the years have usually faced strong incentives not to bring all of the negative facts about West Virginia to the attention of voters, or anyone else, but instead to put the most positive possible spin on their own accomplishments, or claimed accomplishments, and then have their successors in office take the blame for problems. Voters as CEOs must not allow elected officials to get away with this. A recent report by the West Virginia Center on Budget and Policy, "Accountability and Transparency in the West Virginia Budget Process," describes the failure of our state to provide transparency. According to this report, West Virginia is one of the worst states when it comes to providing voters with detailed information about its budget and the decision-making that lies behind the creation of the state's budget. West Virginia is described as being "technologically challenged" as regards the extent to which it makes budget information available online. Voters as CEOs must take the initiative in insisting that West Virginia be steered in the right direction so as to make our state the best in the country as regards transparency.

As regards motivation, it is easy for most voters to play the CEO role because we are mostly free from the sorts of incentives that governors and legislators face. As voters, we really do want to know everything that is wrong with our state so that we can urge that steps be taken by the Governor and the

Legislature to fix those problems. We want this to happen for the sake not only of our own jobs and job prospects, and our standard of living, but also for the well-being of our families, friends, grandchildren, and fellow citizens.

I am not saying that voters are incorruptible, but rather that *as a body* voters are much less corruptible than any smaller constituencies within a state. Voters as individuals can be corrupted, of course, but voters as individuals have virtually no power, and cannot play the CEO role. Voters as members of groups—that is, special interests—can also be corrupted, but these groups have power only if majorities turn a blind eye and allow these groups to get what they want from elected officials who are happy to do favors for special groups of voters in exchange for support at election times. The real power to do good lies with the majority of voters if they choose to exercise that power in the way that a responsible CEO in business exercises power.

The Least Biased Group

Voters as a majority are among the least biased groups in West Virginia, or any state, just because as a group they cannot constitute a special interest. Special interests by definition cannot be majorities. By contrast, an elected official in government may reasonably suppose that if he/she "takes the money and runs" now, making himself and his family better off, this will be best for his own children and grandchildren in the future as well. Voters as majorities are never in a situation anything like this. What is good for them as a group—as a majority, and the larger the majority the better, and especially when they are thinking of their friends or children and grandchildren, as most are—stands a much better chance of being what is genuinely best for West Virginia than is the case regarding elected officials. What I am saying, then, is that voters should begin to think of themselves as exercising a CEO-like role in government, but as members of a potential majority. We should put a lot of effort into figuring out what is best for the state as a whole, and for the long term—and if we do this, we are the more likely to find that many other voters agree with us.

If we voters think of ourselves as playing a CEO-like role where state government is concerned, then where does that leave the elected officials who actually are the government? Answer: We should think of them as being like the heads of divisions and departments in a large company, or in other words the people who most immediately take orders from the CEO. We voters, acting as a majority, and the larger the better, as I said, should convey our wishes to our elected officials, whose job should be to carry out our wishes (within the constraints of state and federal statutes and constitutional limitations, needless to say). After all, everyone knows that elected officials are *public servants*.

Because we all know that elected officials are public servants, it may seem that what I am suggesting here is not a new idea. However, it is a new idea because I am suggesting that we give up the old partisan view of voters where their primary allegiance is to their interests as members of various voting blocks, and where the aim of voters is to have "public servants" serve those interests. The old partisan view makes possible the system that allows government to go on conducting "politics as usual," where the number one goal of politicians is to make promises to a large enough number of sizable voting blocks that a winning strategy can be put together at election time. I am saying that we should replace voters as partisans who look out for their own interests with voters as CEOs where voters look at the larger picture, and instruct elected officials to do what is best for the state as a whole, now and into the future. Here in West Virginia, we should focus on making our state the best in the country—the most prosperous and the best all-around place to live.

Can This Be Made To Work?

Yes, it can, through exposure to the truth on as large a scale as possible. For example, when a majority of voters become familiar with statistics that show how much West Virginia lags behind other states in measures of prosperity, health, graduation rates, etc., and that show also the extent to which West Virginia is not as business-friendly as numerous other states, these same voters will instruct state government to make the necessary changes. Because West Virginia is a wonderful state with many natural advantages, it absolutely does not need to lag behind any other state. "Politics as usual," even when we have an essentially good governor, as we had with Governor Manchin, and good legislators such as we have at present, will not get the job done. Voters as CEOs must play an important role as well.

On the national scene, likewise, a majority of voters must come to understand that if the United States does not begin immediately to make itself much more competitive within the global economy, it will sink under the weight of its debt. Opportunities for success and happiness on the part of nearly everyone will greatly diminish. Voters as CEOs at the national level need to familiarize themselves with comparative information that shows how business-unfriendly the Unites States is—with its high taxes (its corporate tax rate is among the highest in the world, for example), huge compliance costs for meeting tax obligations and conforming to a myriad of regulations, and many other burdens. As I have insisted in earlier chapters, the only good option in any country for dealing with a gargantuan national debt and other large financial commitments is for the country as a whole to make a lot of money by having a strong economy, while simultaneously taking steps to control government spending. But the only proven way to have a strong economy is to strengthen capitalism. And there is no time to lose. Voters as CEOs who understand this will instruct the federal government to make the necessary changes. Because economic success for West Virginia depends in substantial measure on economic success for the country as a whole, West Virginia voters as CEOs also need to be American voters as CEOs.

What About Disagreements Among Voters?

An important question that applies to both state and federal government is the following: Won't voters end up disagreeing among themselves, and between voting blocks, and never arrive at any majority views that will lead to the reforms that are urgently needed in West Virginia and the U.S. as a whole?

My reply to this question is to say first that, up until now, the gloomy answer would probably have been yes. West Virginia and the country as a whole have in the past mostly experienced "politics as usual" on the part of voters as well as politicians. But times have changed. They really have. Voters have become much better informed, partly as a result of the Internet and other expanded informational media in the 21st century, and partly because West Virginia and the U.S. as a whole are still feeling the effects of a severe economic downturn that got everyone's full attention. Voters are highly motivated to learn what must be done to improve our state's and our country's economies. In addition, voters are more interested in the moral dimension of public life than in the past. A new moral consciousness is emerging for both the public and private sectors.

I believe that the time has come when sufficient numbers of people will pay attention to a book such as the one that you holding in your hands. As I have said repeatedly, this book is intended to defend capitalism in a new way that reaches out to Democrats, Republicans, Independents, and everyone else. I hope to have shown in this book that genuine reform for West Virginia and the U.S. requires that the state and the country move toward a much greater reliance than at present on the incentives of capitalism. In the past, the defense of capitalism has mostly been a partisan effort (by Republicans most often, by libertarians also, and sometimes by Democrats), which is exactly why my New Direction for Capitalism is needed so much at the present time. As readers will have seen by now, my primary goal in this book is to transform the defense of capitalism into a largely nonpartisan effort. My goal is to reach out to members of all political groups. I want to unite people, not divide them, by getting them to focus on what matters the most for our state and our country.

Is my goal realistic?

Readers should judge for themselves. Please keep in mind that I am not seeking any greater level of agreement among voters than is necessary for West Virginia to make good on the slogan **Low Taxes, Least Red Tape, Highest Ethics**, and for the U.S. to make the most of its economic potential. My goal in this book is not to promote anything like a complete package of conservative ideas, or liberal ideas, or libertarian ideas, or Tea Party ideas, or Republican ideas, or Democratic ideas. What I am promoting is a "complete package" of those economic and moral ideas required for urgently needed reforms—but it is a much smaller package than any of the other packages to which I just referred. It is both a smaller package of ideas, and a package for which agreement is much easier to achieve. It is a package of core ideas for which a strong case can be made once we look carefully at economic theory, economic history, moral philosophy, and motivational psychology.

The other packages of ideas that I just mentioned—the larger packages (those belonging to liberals, conservatives, libertarians, etc.)—contain a great many valuable components. I am not at all suggesting that voters should not also fight for their favored components, whether these voters are Republicans, Democrats, libertarians, or members of other groups. I am saying only that in this book I do not want to do such a thing. I am aiming for a broader consensus—the sort of consensus needed for voters to be CEOs. This should come first. It is my hope that voters who fight for their own favored larger packages of ideas will first and foremost be part of the consensus required for bringing into existence the important reforms outlined in this book.

A Reference Book For Ceos

As I see it, West Virginia voters have always needed, but did not have until now, anything like a reference book, or manual, for carrying out the duties that belong to voters as CEOs. I would like to believe that West Virginia voters now have such a manual, namely this book, because it does reach out to all groups.

My New Direction for Capitalism is a version of capitalism—and a way of life—that virtually everyone can support. Economically, NDC rests on a solid foundation provided by economic theory and economic history. Morally, NDC rests on the most basic and important of all moral insights, namely that every human being has an intrinsic worth and dignity. This insight is the basis for the version of Universal Moral Pluralism that I spell out in Chapter 8. Politically and socially, NDC rests on unimpeachable conclusions drawn from the study of how various types of incentives actually shape human behavior across a wide range of human activities.

Both Conservatives And Liberals Can Support NDC

NDC's insistence on the need for strictly limited government that protects basic rights and supports free markets should appeal to conservatives. The fact that the moral underpinnings of NDC include moral principles addressed to helping people in need and working toward improving society as a whole should appeal to liberals as well. For NDC, government should not be so limited that it does not contain an adequate safety net for people who are genuinely in need and unable to help themselves. At the same time, NDC is sensitive to the all-important requirement that every government safety net program absolutely must meet: Such programs must contain incentives for people to better their own condition through their own efforts, and these incentives must be strong enough to prevent people from losing out on opportunities to become more self-sufficient through their own efforts even though they are receiving help from the government. This emphasis on self-sufficiency should appeal to both conservatives and liberals.

If welfare programs exist, as they should (all liberals and most conservatives will agree on this point), some degree of welfare dependency on the part of recipients is inevitable. This is unfortunate but unavoidable. NDC emphasizes a balanced approach where welfare dependency is minimized. This approach should appeal strongly to both liberals and conservatives. NDC also emphasizes the autonomy aspect of improving welfare programs, which should find favor with liberals as well as conservatives: Whenever possible, people in need who cannot adequately care for themselves should be given money to help meet their needs (but with the right sorts of progressive incentives built into the programs to encourage the people receiving the money to improve their condition by earning money themselves if they are able to do so). However, the responsibility for how to spend the money should largely be left with the people themselves, thus ensuring that the autonomy of these people is not undermined. As much as possible, welfare support for people in need should not be demeaning to these people and should encourage them to improve their own condition.

For NDC, incentives make the world go round, as I have said. The acid test for any program or political or social system is whether or not it contains incentives that actually work in support of basic moral principles. This emphasis on creating the best incentives in both the private and public sectors should appeal to both conservatives and liberals, as well as to people who would describe themselves as being partly conservative and partly liberal. The emphasis placed by NDC on human autonomy—as regards all domains of life—should likewise appeal to both conservatives and liberals, and to everyone in between, as should the importance assigned by NDC to protecting basic freedoms such as speech, press, and assembly. For NDC, everyone ought to be accorded respect regardless of their race, gender, age, national origin, religious belief (or absence of religious belief), economic standing, sexual orientation, or extent of physical or mental handicap. People who are accused of crimes, along with those who are convicted of crimes, also ought to be accorded respect.

Most people in West Virginia and elsewhere, whether they

are liberals or conservatives or fall somewhere in between, should look favorably upon the fact that NDC rejects all attempts to defend free markets by appealing to egoism or to the idea that the only responsibility of people in business is to make as much profit as possible. Most people everywhere will judge that any such appeals are flat-out unacceptable, and for an excellent reason—they are not consistent with basic moral principles entailed by the intrinsic value of all human lives. At the same time, NDC is completely realistic in recognizing that for people who *are* motivated wholly or largely by self-interest (and of course a significant number of people do fall into this category) the best economic system for reigning in their self-interest and ensuring that it will also serve the good of others, insofar as this is possible, is capitalism.

The conclusion that I want to reach at this point in the discussion is that voters do not need to end up disagreeing among themselves, or between voting blocks, in such fashion as to undermine the sort of agreement among them that is required for voters as CEOs to push for reforms that are urgently needed in West Virginia and the United States as a whole. As a starting point in seeking agreement among themselves, voters can refer to ideas that are defended in this book.

Can Voters Really Be Ceos?

In referring to the "voters as CEOs" view of democratic government, I do not mean to suggest that voters should attempt to involve themselves in the day-to-day running of government, or anything like that. They should instead genuinely compare themselves to CEOs at the very top in the chain of command at large corporations, as opposed to factory or office managers, or heads of divisions or major departments in a corporation. The latter can all be likened to elected officials, who do, after all, run the country on a day-to-day basis. What, then, does the CEO of a large corporation do? Well, sometimes he/she will take the time to learn in detail what a particular division is doing day-to-day, especially if there is a problem. But mainly, the CEO looks at the larger picture, and this is what voters should do. As I have noted, business CEOs spend a lot of time looking at comparative reports: how the corporation's sales, indebtedness, capitalization, access to resources, etc., compare to like measures for other companies. Business CEOs spend a lot of time addressing questions such as the following: Is the company planning well for the future in areas such as product design and marketing? Does the company have in place a good business system that motivates employees in the best ways? Is it anticipating any possible future shortages of skilled employees? Is routine maintenance being carried out properly for all of the company's buildings and equipment? When will the company's facilities need to be renovated or replaced, and how will this be accomplished? Will the company have adequate capital to carry through on all of its projects?

How do questions such as these apply to government? Let us consider the example of routine maintenance.

All across the United States, a great many roads, bridges, dams, levees, and underground pipes are deteriorating. West Virginia is notorious for its bad city streets and rural roads, and its past-their-prime bridges. According to the American Society of Civil Engineers, as of 2010 39% of bridges in West Virginia were structurally deficient or obsolete. All across the state and the country, infrastructure is not being given the maintenance that is needed, nor are structures being replaced in a timely fashion when this is called for.

Why?

The answer is simple: Both the federal government and our

state government are short on money, so elected officials all to often simply cross their fingers and hope that nothing really bad happens on their watch. This enables them to use available money to conduct "politics as usual" by supporting projects that are more visible than infrastructure maintenance or replacement. Building a *new* highway or transit system—that is a project that people will notice, officials believe, and also will garner a lot of votes from the people in the vicinity of the new highway or transit system who will directly benefit. But is the new highway or transit system the best use *overall* for taxpayers' money? Is it the fairest use for taxpayers' money? These are questions that people in government usually do not want to ask, even when the answers are *yes*, since their main concern is with pleasing the special interests that will benefit directly from the new project. Because politicians care much less about the more diffuse interests of people all across the state or country, they pay insufficient attention to infrastructure maintenance and replacement.

From what I have said in the previous paragraph, focusing on only one type of example, readers should be able to get a sense for just how inadequate elected officials typically are when they are called upon to function as bona fide CEOs in running a state or a country. For a CEO in the business world, by contrast, routine maintenance and timely replacement for a company's facilities are at the top of the CEO's to-do list since they play such obvious roles in regard to the company's future profitability. Yet, *someone* ought to perform the parallel functions of a CEO in running a state or a country. If not elected officials, then who will do it? You know what my answer is: Voters should do it—once they come together as a majority who want the state or country to be run properly now and into the future. There is no other good option.

Epilogue.
What West Virginians Can Do

West Virginia has the potential for becoming the best state in the country—the most prosperous, the nicest, the safest, and the all-around best place to live. What can West Virginians do to ensure that this comes to pass?

The most important thing for you to do is adopt the "voters as CEOs" mind set described in the previous chapter. The fate of West Virginia is in the hands of its voters. The "voters as CEOs" mind set will be effective for our state only if a majority of voters in West Virginia support the sorts of reforms that are required for West Virginia to become the best state in the U.S. West Virginia absolutely must become thoroughly business-friendly, and it must become a state where all people are treated well regardless of their place within society.

Great things can be accomplished via consensus. If large numbers of West Virginians come to support more or less the same core set of capitalistic reforms, this fact in itself will go a long way toward making West Virginia the most prosperous state in the country since it will reassure people in business in a way that nothing else can reassure them. It will provide sound reasons for business people, both within the state and outside the state, to believe that reforms in West Virginia will be long-lasting. West Virginia will be unique among all the states.

At the present time in all 50 states, including West Virginia, there is nothing like widespread agreement as regards basic ideas for capitalistic reforms. More to the point, the political process across the nation has to a great extent been reduced to conflicts among various interest groups and voting blocks, as opposed to being a search for the best people to serve in government, and the best reforms for making government better. Among all of the states, West Virginia has the best chance to move beyond all of the dissension because West Virginia is small and has long possessed a sense of solidarity among its people that is rare. If the people of any state can come together to accomplish important tasks, West Virginians can. If the people of any state can find the will to enact new policies that are economically sound and morally praiseworthy, and do so quickly, West Virginians can.

About the Author

Ralph William Clark is Professor and Chair of the Philosophy Department and Coordinator of the Humanities Program at West Virginia University, where he has taught for nearly 40 years. He was born in Exeter, New Hampshire, and lived as a child on Plum Island, Massachusetts. He received his B.A., Phi Beta Kappa, from the University of Denver and his Ph.D. from the University of Colorado. He is coauthor of *A Good Day's Work: Sustaining Ethical Behavior and Business Success*. He has three grown children—two sons and one stepson—and one grandchild. Dr. Clark lives in Morgantown with his wife Suzanne.

*The views expressed in this book are those of the author,
and not West Virginia University.*